educamos·sm

Caro aluno, seja bem-vindo à sua plataforma do conhecimento!

A partir de agora, você tem à sua disposição uma plataforma que reúne, em um só lugar, recursos educacionais digitais que complementam os livros impressos e são desenvolvidos especialmente para auxiliar você em seus estudos. Veja como é fácil e rápido acessar os recursos deste projeto.

1 Faça a ativação dos códigos dos seus livros.

Se você NÃO tiver cadastro na plataforma:

- Para acessar os recursos digitais, você precisa estar cadastrado na plataforma educamos.sm. Em seu computador, acesse o endereço <br.educamos.sm>.
- No canto superior direito, clique em "**Primeiro acesso? Clique aqui**". Para iniciar o cadastro, insira o código indicado abaixo.
- Depois de incluir todos os códigos, clique em "**Registrar-se**" e, em seguida, preencha o formulário para concluir esta etapa.

Se você JÁ fez cadastro na plataforma:

- Em seu computador, acesse a plataforma e faça o *login* no canto superior direito.
- Em seguida, você visualizará os livros que já estão ativados em seu perfil. Clique no botão "**Adicionar livro**" e insira o código abaixo.

Este é o seu código de ativação! → **DZ4N3-BQTBR-APJ7P**

I WORLD ING 2 (LA) ED 2018

2 Acesse os recursos.

Usando um computador

Acesse o endereço <br.educamos.sm> e faça o *login* no canto superior direito. Nessa página, você visualizará todos os seus livros cadastrados. Para acessar o livro desejado, basta clicar na sua capa.

Usando um dispositivo móvel

Instale o aplicativo **educamos.sm**, que está disponível gratuitamente na loja de aplicativos do dispositivo. Utilize o mesmo *login* e a mesma senha da plataforma para acessar o aplicativo.

Importante! Não se esqueça de sempre cadastrar seus livros da SM em seu perfil. Assim, você garante a visualização dos seus conteúdos, seja no computador, seja no dispositivo móvel. Em caso de dúvida, entre em contato com nosso atendimento pelo **telefone 0800 72 54876** ou pelo **e-mail** atendimento@grupo-sm.com.

07009

Letter to the Student

Dear Student,

Welcome to **i-World**!

i-World is a modern, dynamic course that gives you a truly blended approach to learning. It integrates online activities with classroom materials to provide you with the 21st century skills necessary for the world outside the classroom. **i-World** will help you communicate effectively in all modern-day situations.

In your *Student's Book*, you will find:
- A broad variety of authentic content and topics to help develop your language.
- Communicative activities that you can relate to your own experience.
- A focus on modern-day issues that helps you compare ideas.
- Continuous opportunities for project work and cooperative learning.

About your *Student's Book*:

Your *Student's Book* has a Welcome unit and eight regular units. Each regular unit is divided into three sections:
- *My World* introduces you to the topic of the unit.
- *Views* relates to people's personal experiences about the topic.
- *Out and About* provides cultural information from around the world related to the topic.

Each section contains reading, listening, speaking, and writing activities to help you develop all four skills. The units end with a review page for practice of language and vocabulary.

At the back of your book, you will find *Pairwork* activities that are relevant to certain units, group *Projects*, a *Grammar Reference*, a *Phonetic Symbols* table, an *Irregular Verbs* list, and a *Workbook*.

We at University of Dayton Publishing sincerely believe that **i-World** will provide you with a solid foundation in English and enable you to progress in a positive way.

Get ready to explore the world with **i-World**.

Your gateway to a digital world!

Our new virtual learning environment will provide you with all the interactive practice you need. On **educamos·sm**, you will find:

Interactive activities for practice and consolidation.

Videos of communicative situations.

An *Online Reader* with comprehension activities.

Don't forget— **educamos·sm** is also where you can find our *Online Worksite* for even more practice!

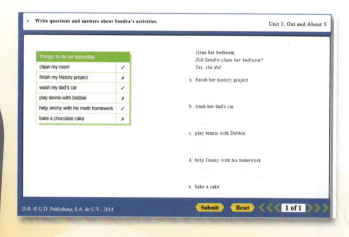

Look for and click on these icons in your *Digital Book*:

 Online Reader
 Online practice activities
Videos
World Book Online Encyclopedia links

Contents

Unit	Grammar	Vocabulary	Reading
Welcome p. 6	Review of personal information Simple Present review Present Continuous review	My Community	Personal information A quiz
1 World of English p. 12	Simple Present *To be* Imperatives *There is/There are*	Countries and nationalities Cardinal and ordinal numbers Classroom objects	An encyclopedia entry A letter A magazine article
2 A Typical Day p. 22	Simple Present (Affirmative and Negative) Simple Present (Questions and Short Answers) Adverbs of Frequency	Telling the time Leisure activities Chores	A website A survey A magazine article
3 My Favorites p. 32	Expressing Likes and Dislikes Expressing Likes and Dislikes (3rd Person Singular) Possessive Adjectives	School subjects Clothes	Articles
4 Something Special p. 42	*Whose* and Possessive Pronouns *What/How about* + Noun or Gerund *How long does it take?*	Skateboarding Ordinals 20th-100th Special places	Profiles Text messages A magazine article
5 Animal Antics p. 52	Gerunds (-ing) Infinitives (Purpose) Present Continuous	Action verbs Animals Prepositions of place	A web article A profile A magazine article
6 The USA p. 62	*To be* (Simple Past and Past Continuous) Simple Past (Regular Verbs) Simple Past (Negative, Questions, and Short Answers)	Dates Jobs Cognates	A brochure A biography A magazine article
7 Story Time p. 72	Relative Clauses (*Who/That/Where*) Simple Past (Irregular Verbs) Past Time Clauses with *When*	Sequencing words Adjective opposites Conjunctions	A book summary A story A magazine article
8 Feeling Good p. 82	Countable and Uncountable Nouns (*Some/Any*) Adverbs of Manner Making Suggestions	Food Parts of the body Weather	Magazine articles An instruction leaflet

Listening	Speaking	Writing
Meeting people A school project	Meeting people at a party	A school-to-school message
Conversations Instructions	A conversation An interview **Pronunciation**: The alphabet	Rules A picture dictionary
A discussion An interview	Information gaps A survey **Pronunciation**: /s/, /iz/, and /z/	A chat A weekly planner
Survey results Conversations	A survey A conversation **Pronunciation**: /i/ vs /i:/	Lists A magazine article An online opinion
Conversations Instructions	Conversations **Pronunciation**: Expressing emotions	Chat A description
A conversation A radio program A profile	A description **Pronunciation**: Syllable stress	A profile
A guided tour A radio program A game show	A game A history quiz **Pronunciation**: /t/, /d/, and /id/	A biography
A book summary Stories	A consensus Stories **Pronunciation**: Rhythm	Stories
Instructions A conversation	An explanation A role-play **Pronunciation**: /æ/ and /ʌ/	Instructions A description

Pairwork 92
Projects 96
Grammar Reference 104
Phonetic Symbols 110
Irregular Verbs 111
Workbook 112

Contents 5

Welcome Unit

My World

Reading > Personal Information

1 Read the intranet site and write one word for each category.

Countries	
Nationalities	

School subjects	
Sports	

 Summerville Camp Intranet

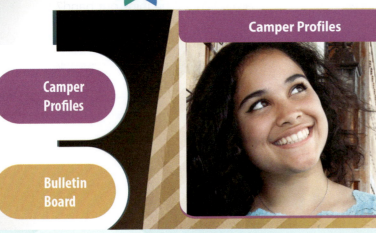

Camper Profiles

Camper Profiles

Bulletin Board

Hi, I'm Amanda and I'm in the Dance Program 10G. My parents are Mexican, but I'm from the US. My favorite school subjects are English and history. My hobbies are playing tennis and listening to music. I don't like writing, but I love reading. My favorite author is George R. R. Martin. He's great!

2 Work in pairs. Ask questions to complete the table with your partner's information.

Name: _____   Age: _____

Favorite subjects: _____

Likes: _____

Dislikes: _____

Listening > Meeting People

1 Work in pairs. Look at the picture and answer the questions.

  a. What are they doing?
  b. Where are they from?
  c. Do you think they are friends? Why or why not?

2 Listen and check your answers.

3 Listen again and write Brianna's information.

  Place of birth: _____

  Favorite school subjects: _____

  Hobbies: _____

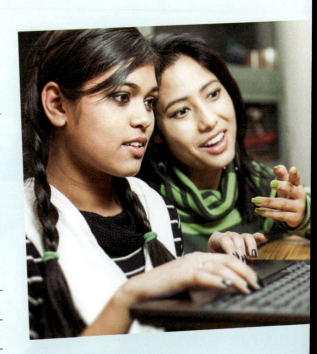

Grammar › Review of Personal Information

1 Mark which sentences give personal information *P* or talk about abilities *A*.

a. *I'm Sandy.* ___
b. *I could teach you!* ___
c. *We're the same age!* ___
d. *My grandparents are from Boston.* ___
e. *Can you play the guitar?* ___
f. *I can't play the guitar.* ___

2 Unscramble the sentences and complete the invitation.

a. you / 14 or 15 / ? / are / years old
b. in the Dance / you / ? / are / or Sports Program
c. instrument / can / you / a musical / ? / play
d. ? / you / can / sing

3 Complete the party conversation.

HELEN: Hi Paul! 1) _____
PAUL: I'm good, thanks.
HELEN: Who's your friend?
PAUL: 2) _____ Jerome. He's new in the camp.
HELEN: 3) _____ from?
PAUL: Paris. He's a musician.
 4) _____ the piano really well!
HELEN: What if he joins our band?
 5) _____ the guitar?
PAUL: I don't know. Let me introduce you!

4 Write the questions Helen asks Jerome.

a. (how old)
_____
b. (what instruments / play)
_____
c. (can / sing)
_____
d. (who / favorite singer)
_____
e. (what / your favorite band)
_____

Speaking › Meeting People at a Party

1 Write questions to ask people you meet in a party.

a. _____
b. _____
c. _____
d. _____

2 Work in groups. Ask and answer with other students.

Welcome Unit 7

Views

Reading > A Quiz

1 Read and answer the quiz.

2 Work in groups. Discuss the questions.
   a. Do you agree with the results of the quiz?
   b. How similar are you and your best friend?

FUN CAMP

This Week's Quiz

Good friends don't always like the same things. What do you do with your best friend? Are you ideal friends or not? Try our quiz to find out!

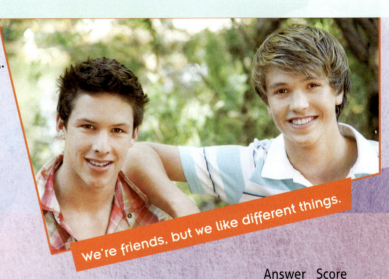

We're friends, but we like different things.

Answer   Score

1. **How often do you see your friend?**
   a) A few days a week.   b) Once a month.   c) Every day.

2. **Do you visit your friend's house?**
   a) Never.   b) It's like home!   c) A few times.

3. **What's your friend's family like?**
   a) Friendly.   b) Like my family.   c) I don't know them.

4. **What happens when you meet a friend of your friend?**
   a) I ignore them.   b) What other friend?   c) We become friends after some time.

5. **Do you know your friend's favorite food?**
   a) No idea!   b) Of course!   c) I don't need to know.

6. **Do you and your friend have many jokes only you understand?**
   a) No, why?   b) Yeah, some!   c) Ha-ha, obviously!

7. **Does your friend trust you?**
   a) I think so.   b) I'm not sure.   c) Sometimes.

8. **What do you call your friend?**
   a) By his/her name.   b) It depends.   c) His/her nickname.

Total

Score
1. a) 1   b) 0   c) 2
2. a) 0   b) 2   c) 1
3. a) 1   b) 2   c) 0
4. a) 1   b) 0   c) 2
5. a) 0   b) 2   c) 1
6. a) 0   b) 1   c) 2
7. a) 2   b) 0   c) 1
8. a) 0   b) 1   c) 2

Results
14–16: It looks like you're clones! Don't you get bored together?

7–13: Your balance is perfect. You are ideal friends!

6 or below: You don't have many things in common. Are you sure you are friends?

Welcome Unit

Grammar > Simple Present Review

1 Read the extracts and mark the sentences.
✓ = affirmative   ✗ = negative   ? = question

a. *Do you visit your friend's house?* ___
b. *We like different things.* ___
c. *What do you call your friend?* ___
d. *You don't have many things in common.* ___
e. *I ignore them.* ___
f. *I don't know them.* ___

2 Match the questions with the answers.
a. When do we use simple present?
b. What do we add to the verb when we use *he, she,* and *it*?
c. What auxiliary verb do we use for questions?
d. How do we modify the main verb when we use the auxiliary?
e. Where do you put the subject in questions?

___ Between the auxiliary and the verb.
___ *Do* or *does*.
___ To talk about habits/routines and facts.
___ We don't, the verb is in its base form.
___ *-s* or *-es*.

3 Complete the pen pal profile with the correct form of the verbs in the box.

go   hate   have   not like
play   read   think   watch

Name: Aaron
Age: 16
From:

Description: Hello, I am from Hungary. I speak Hungarian and English. I 1) _____ books and 2) _____ movies and TV series in my free time. I like comics, but I 3) _____ manga or anime. My best friend is Rob. We 4) _____ to the same school and we 5) _____ a band. He 6) _____ the drums and I sing. He 7) _____ singing! Please write to me if you 8) _____ we can become pen pals!

Contact this person

4 Use the prompts to write questions for Aaron.
a. (brothers or sisters) _____
_____
b. (favorite TV series) _____
_____
c. (kind of band) _____
_____
d. (like sports) _____
_____

Out and About

Vocabulary > My Community

1 Mark the statements according to what the people are talking about: *C* celebrations, *P* places in their community, *T* transport.

a. My town has really good buses. ___

b. Carnival in my city is fun! ___

c. The local history museum is very interesting. ___

d. Taxis are very expensive. ___

e. We have parades at Christmas. ___

f. We sometimes go to the mall after school. ___

2 Write three words for each group.

Places in a town _____

_____

Transport _____

_____

Celebrations _____

_____

Writing > A School-to-School Message

> Choose one of the topics: technology, food, or houses. Write a paragraph about your country for students in another country.

Listening > A School Project

1 Work in pairs. Describe the potential problems for communication via Internet.

- lost connection
- sound not clear
- no picture
- time difference

2 Listen and circle the problem the students are having.

3 Listen again and underline the correct options.

a. Louis is studying *history / geography / art*.

b. He is *painting / making a mask / drawing*.

c. Melissa's project is about *animals / festivals / plants*.

d. She asks Louis for a picture of *Mardi Gras / his family / his pets*.

10 Welcome Unit

Grammar › Present Continuous Review

1 Read the extracts and answer the questions.

> What are you doing?
> He's listening to you.
> Are you painting?
> No, I'm not.
> I'm not wearing a costume.
> I'm working on my geography project.

a. When do we use the present continuous?
   _____

b. How do we form negative sentences?
   _____

c. How does the word order change in questions?
   _____

d. How does the main verb change?
   _____

2 Look at the Mardi Gras picture below and complete the e-mail.

Hello Melissa,

Here is the picture you need. As you can see, Mardi Gras is fun. People get very excited, here they 1) _____ (waving) to the people in the float. My sister is there, wearing a pink blouse. My dad 2) _____ (shout) at her to say hello. The boy in orange is my brother. He 3) _____ (blow) a horn. It's very noisy. Do you have horns like this in your country?

Let's talk tomorrow. I hope the video is OK now!

Louis

P.S: You can't see me in the picture, but I 4) _____ (wear) the mask from my art class!

3 Use the prompts to write what people in the picture are doing.

a. (carry a baby)
   _____

b. (juggle)
   _____

c. (eat apple)
   _____

d. (take a photo)
   _____

e. (laugh)
   _____

Welcome Unit 11

1 World of English

Value Commitment Commitment is an act, not a word

1 Number the reasons for learning English in order of importance.
- [ ] Listen to music
- [ ] Watch movies
- [ ] Use the Internet
- [ ] Make new friends
- [ ] Find out about the world
- [ ] Travel
- [ ] Learn new things

2 Work in groups. Compare your lists.

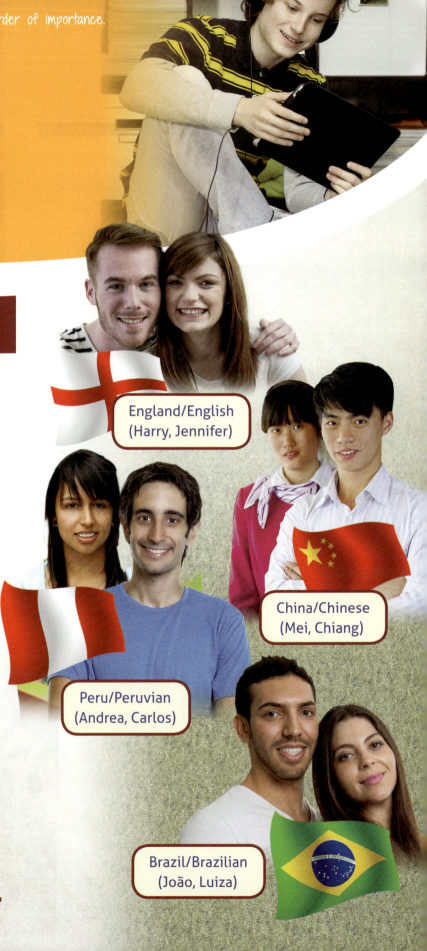

England/English (Harry, Jennifer)

China/Chinese (Mei, Chiang)

Peru/Peruvian (Andrea, Carlos)

Brazil/Brazilian (João, Luiza)

WHAT'S IN A NAME?

Names identify people, animals, places, and things. Every person has a name. In the US, most people have three names—a first name, a middle name, and a last name. The last name is also called the family name.

FIRST NAMES

The popularity of different names is constantly shifting. Nowadays, some popular first names in the United States are Liam and Mason for boys, and Sophia and Isabella for girls. They are from different languages. Liam is Irish, Mason is French, Sophia is Greek, and Isabella is Spanish. Other popular names are from Asia or Africa. Many first names have special meanings. For example, Naomi is Japanese and means "beautiful," Alexander means "defender," and Richard means "brave."

LAST NAMES

Last names often come from locations, occupations, or people's physical appearance. For example, the family name Hill means "a person who lives near a hill." Gardener and Cook are occupations. Short, Long, and Little are descriptions of people's physical qualities. There are also many non-English family names in the US. The biggest group is Hispanic. There are thirteen Hispanic family names in the first 100 most common last names.

12 Unit 1

My World

Reading > What's in a name?

> **Thinking about the Topic**
> Before reading, think about what you know about the topic. This helps you to understand the text.

1. Work in pairs. Answer the questions.
   a. How many names do you have?
   b. What is the meaning of your name?

2. Read the encyclopedia entry on page 12 and write the language of origin of each name.
   a. Sophia _____
   b. Liam _____
   c. Mason _____
   d. Naomi _____

3. Underline the correct options to complete the sentences.
   a. Most people in the US have…
      1. a first name and two last names.
      2. a first, a middle, and a last name.
   b. *Liam* is…
      1. a last name.
      2. a first name.
   c. The last name Cook gives information about…
      1. a person's appearance.
      2. where a person lives.
      3. a person's occupation.
   d. In the US, thirteen of the top 100 last names are…
      1. Hispanic.
      2. Asian.
      3. Greek.

4. Work in pairs. List last names in your language that indicate locations, occupations, or physical appearance.

Vocabulary > Countries and Nationalities

1. Refer to the encyclopedia entry and complete the introductions.
   a. My name's João. I'm _____.
   b. I'm from China. Mei is a _____ name.
   c. I'm Andrea. I'm from _____.
   d. My name's Harry. I'm _____.

2. Work in pairs. Write a list of countries and corresponding nationalities. Share your list with another pair.

Listening > Registration Day

1. Work in pairs. Look at the registration form. Say what it is for and give your own information.

Student Registration Form

First name: Brianna

Last name:

Nationality: American

Age:

Address:

Telephone number:

2. John and Brianna are registering for a class. Listen and complete the form for Brianna.

3. Listen again and mark the sentences *T* (true) or *F* (false).
   a. The boy's name is John. ____
   b. He and Brianna are there to register for a French class. ____
   c. His friends are from Scotland and from Canada. ____
   d. The registrar speaks to John. ____

Unit 1 13

Grammar > Simple Present *to be*

1 Read the examples from *Track 4*. Match the responses to the questions.

> *Are you Irish?* ___
> *Are they your friends?* ___
> *Is the girl from Scotland?* ___
> *Are we in the right line?* ___
> *How old are you?* ___
> *What's your address?* ___
>
> See *Grammar Reference*, page 104.

a. Yes, they are.
b. No, I'm not. I'm American.
c. 1022 Washington Avenue.
d. Yes, we are.
e. No, she isn't. She's from Canada.
f. I'm fourteen.

2 Underline the forms of *to be* in the examples.

3 Underline the correct options to complete the conversations in the opposite column.

Speaking > Registering for a Class

> Complete the registration card. In pairs, ask and answer questions to register for a language course.

INSTANT LANGUAGE ACADEMY
REGISTRATION FORM

First name

Age

Middle name

Nationality

Last name

Telephone number

Address

a. *Is/Are* you from France?

Yes, I *am/are*.

b. *Are/Is* she Spanish?

No, she *aren't/isn't*.

c. *Is/Are* they American?

No, they *are/aren't*.

d. *Is/Are* we in the same class?

Yes, we *are/aren't*.

e. How old *is/are* you?
I *am/She is* fifteen.

f. *What/How* is your address?
179 West Road.

14 Unit 1

Views

Listening ▸ First Day of School

Using Visual Information
Before listening, use visual clues from pictures to identify the topic.

1. Look at the phrases on the board and underline the topic.
   a. Homework
   b. Class schedule
   c. Class rules

2. Listen to the teacher talking and check your answer.

3. Listen again and underline the correct answers.
   a. What is the teacher's last name?
      1. Jonson.   2. Jones.   3. Johnson.
   b. Where are the rules?
      1. On the blackboard.   2. On the wall.   3. On the whiteboard.
   c. What time is the first class?
      1. At 8:00.   2. At 9:00.   3. At 8:30.
   d. Which is the most important rule for the teacher?
      1. Arrive on time.   2. Do your homework.   3. Only speak English in class.

Pronunciation ▸ The Alphabet

1. Listen to the pronunciation of the vowel sounds. Then categorize the letters of the alphabet according to their vowel sound.

   A B C D E F G H I J K L M N O P Q R S T U V W X Y Z

/eɪ/ (eight)	
/iː/ (he)	
/e/ (spell)	
/aɪ/ (I)	
/əʊ/ (no)	
/uː/ (blue)	
/ɑː/ (are)	

2. Listen and check your answers.

3. Work in pairs. Practice saying the initials. Then list initials for things in your country and say them aloud.
   a. USA   c. AC/DC   e. FBI
   b. CD   d. VIP   f. OK

Vocabulary ▸ Cardinal and Ordinal Numbers

1. Match the cardinal numbers in the box to the ordinal numbers.

   1 2 3 4 5 9 10 12 13 20

   a. fifth ____   f. third ____
   b. tenth ____   g. fourth ____
   c. second ____   h. twelfth ____
   d. first ____   i. twentieth ____
   e. ninth ____   j. thirteenth ____

2. Take the numbers quiz. Then check your answers in pairs.

   What is…
   a. the third letter of the capital of the USA?
   b. 4 plus 5 plus 10?
   c. the number of letters in your teacher's last name?
   d. your street address?
   e. the telephone number of your school?
   f. your fourth class today?

Unit 1 15

Reading > School Rules

1 Mark (✓) the statements that are true about the rules at your school.
   a. My school has a lot of rules. ___
   b. The rules are on a website. ___
   c. The rules are clear and fair. ___
   d. My parents know the school rules. ___

2 Read the letter and underline who it is for.
   a. Students   b. Parents   c. Students and parents

Dear Students,

Here is a copy of the Glenville Academy Classroom Rules Contract. Read the rules carefully. Take them home, show your parents, and then sign at the bottom. 1) ___

We expect all students to follow these rules. They are very important.
a. Arrive on time. Three tardies equal one absence.
b. Be prepared. Bring your schoolbooks, notebooks, and pens every day.
c. Bring gym clothes for P.E. 2) ___
d. Do not work on homework in class. Homework is for home!
e. Show respect for teachers and other students. Talk politely and listen carefully.
f. Do not shout or jump around in class. 3) ___
g. Do not use your cell phone without permission. 4) ___
h. Do not eat food in the classroom. There is a cafeteria for snacks.

Student signature: ....
Date: ....

Parent/Guardian signature: ....
Date: ....

Thank you for your cooperation.

The Principal

3 Label the missing sentences below in the text.
   a. Keep them turned off!
   b. Put your hand up to ask a question.
   c. Return the signed copy to your homeroom teacher.
   d. Students without the appropriate clothing cannot attend class.

4 Work in groups. Discuss the questions.
   a. Which rules are the same in your school? Which are different?
   b. Which school rules are more important?
   c. Does your school need more rules? Why? Why not?

Grammar > Imperatives

1 Read the examples from the letter. Mark the sentences *P* (positive) or *N* (negative).

> *Bring gym clothes for P.E.* ___
> *Do not shout in class.* ___
> *Arrive on time.* ___
> *Do not use your cell phone.* ___
>
> See *Grammar Reference*, page 104.

2 Mark (✓) the correct options to complete the rules.

a. We use the imperative to…

___ give instructions.

___ ask for information.

b. To form imperatives, we use the…

___ base form of the verb.

___ *-ing* form of the verb.

c. To form negative imperatives, the main verb follows…

___ are not.

___ do not.

3 Mark (✓) the appropriate options to complete the rules for a class poster.

a. ___ Eat
   ___ Don't eat
   in class.

b. ___ Listen
   ___ Don't listen
   to the teacher.

c. ___ Do
   ___ Don't do
   your homework on time.

d. ___ Write
   ___ Don't write
   your name on your desk.

e. ___ Send
   ___ Don't send
   text messages in class.

4 Write the rules to complete the poster.

a. _____

b. _____   c. _____

d. _____   e. _____

Writing > The Ideal School

1 Work in pairs. Write five rules for your ideal school.

2 Compare your rules with your classmates'.

Out and About

Reading > Digital Classrooms

1. Work in pairs. Look at the pictures and mark (✓) what you can find in a digital classroom.
   a. a blackboard ___
   b. tablets ___
   c. textbooks ___
   d. an interactive whiteboard ___
   e. a cassette player ___
   f. video animations and online games ___

2. Read the article quickly and underline the best title.
   a. No more heavy bags!
   b. Don't forget your books!
   c. A full bag!

3. Answer the questions.
   a. What is in Karim's school bag?
   _____
   b. What is different about Karim's school?
   _____
   c. What kind of technology is there at Karim's school?
   _____
   d. What is Karim's favorite class?
   _____
   e. Why is Karim happy?
   _____

4. Work in pairs. Look at the pictures of the two classrooms again and discuss the similarities and differences between them. Then make notes in the table.

	Advantages	Disadvantages
Traditional classroom		
Digital classroom		

DIGITAL WORLD magazine

What's in your school bag? Are there books and pens? Is there a dictionary or a calculator? School bags are usually big and heavy. They aren't easy to carry. But Karim's bag is different. It isn't full of books and pens and erasers and rulers. There is only one thing in it—a tablet computer. Karim is a student at a digital school in the US.

There are no books at Karim's school. All the students at the school have a tablet computer. There is also an electronic whiteboard in every classroom. The materials for lessons are on students' tablets. There are readings and listenings with animations and video. There are interactive exercises that give

students help when they want it. There is also a special learning platform for students to talk about homework, post assignments, and interact when they work on projects.

Karim's favorite class is English. There are lots of fun learning games, and Karim communicates with students in other schools. He is very happy that there are no more heavy bags to carry!

Vocabulary > Classroom Objects

1. Look at the pictures of the classrooms and label the things you can see.
   a. school bag
   b. pen
   c. pencil
   d. eraser
   e. dictionary
   f. notebook
   g. paper
   h. ruler
   i. calculator

2. Work in pairs. Guess what your partner has in his or her school bag. Make a list.

3. Share your list with your partner. Check how many guesses were correct.

Writing > Around the Classroom

1. Work in pairs. Name more items in your classroom. Use a dictionary to help you.

2. Create a picture dictionary of classroom objects in English.
   - Draw pictures of the objects.
   - Write the words in English.
   - Add translations of the words in your language.

Listening > A New School

1. Listen and underline the correct options to complete the sentences.
   a. There are *fifteen/twenty-five* students in Dan's class.
   b. He *has/doesn't have* computers in the classroom.
   c. The electronic whiteboard is very *old/modern*.
   d. Dan uses *the school library/a tablet*.
   e. The cafeteria is *very/not very* good.

2. Work in pairs. Compare your school to Dan's.
   In our school there is…, but in Dan's there are…

Unit 1   19

Grammar > There is/There are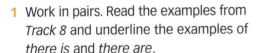

1 Work in pairs. Read the examples from Track 8 and underline the examples of *there is* and *there are*.

> There are computers in the classroom.
> Is there an electronic whiteboard?
> Yes, there is.
> Is there a school library?
> No, there isn't.
>
> See *Grammar Reference*, page 104.

2 Underline the correct options to complete the rules.

a. We use there *is/are* to talk about singular things.

b. We use there *is/are* to talk about plural things.

c. We use *isn't* and *aren't* in *affirmative/negative* statements.

d. The word order *changes/does not change* in questions.

3 Look at the classrooms and complete the exchanges.

Classroom A

A: _____ there a teacher?

B: No, there _____.

A: How many posters _____?

B: There _____ one poster.

A: How many students _____ there?

B: There _____ four.

Classroom B

C: _____ there computers?

D: Yes, there _____.

C: _____ there an electronic whiteboard?

D: _____, there _____.

4 Work in pairs. Ask and answer more questions about the classrooms.

Classroom A

Classroom B

Speaking > The Ideal Classroom

1 Imagine your ideal classroom. Use the prompts to make notes about its features.

- Electronic whiteboard
- Computers
- Posters on the walls
- Dictionaries
- Other

2 Ask and answer questions with your classmates about your ideal classrooms. Find someone whose classroom is the same as yours.

Are there ... in the classroom?
Is there a ... ?

20 Unit 1

Review

1 Look at the picture and complete the information card. Then write information cards for five more famous people you know.

Name:

From:

Nationality:

Age (approx.):

> Imagine you are at a celebrity party. Use the information cards to talk about the people with another student.

Who is he/she?
Where's he/she from?/What nationality is he/she?
How old is he/she?

2 Complete the classroom poster with the verbs in the box.

check   ask   shout   speak   raise

English Class Rules

- 1) _____ for help in English.
- Don't 2) _____ in class.
- 3) _____ your hand to ask a question.
- Don't 4) _____ in Portuguese.
- 5) _____ your spelling in a dictionary.
- _____
- _____

> Add two more rules to the poster.

3 Look at the picture. Write questions and answers with the prompts.

a. a poster on the wall?
   Is there a poster on the wall? Yes, there is.

b. a desk for the teacher?
   _____

c. windows in the classroom?
   _____

d. how many chairs?
   _____

e. a whiteboard?
   _____

> Work in pairs. Ask and answer more questions about the classroom.

4 Read the guidelines from the school's English Club. List the resources for learning English it mentions.

Learning Guidelines

There are lots of resources for learning English today. Of course, there are textbooks and dictionaries, but there is also the Internet. There are social networking sites and sites with magazines, music, and movies online. There are also special sites for learners of English. Use these resources. Keep a vocabulary notebook and write down useful words. Read the lyrics when you listen to music. Watch movies with English subtitles. Show your commitment to learning English!

> Write three things you can do to help you learn English.

Unit 1   21

2 A Typical Day

Value Punctuality Better three hours early than a minute late

1 Work in pairs. Discuss the quote and say whether or not you agree and why.

2 Conduct a class survey to find out if your classmates are usually early, on time, or late for different events.

ST. MARGARET'S BOARDING SCHOOL

Search

| Home | About Us | Parents | Library | Athletics | News | Contact Us |

- School life ▸ Boarding life
- Academic
- Sports
- Activities
- Admissions

by Sally Shore, 10th Grade

My boarding school is my second home. I live here most of the year because my mom and dad travel a lot. Some students here, called day students, go home in the evenings, but most of us are boarders. That means that we sleep and eat at school. I only see my family on school vacations. Just like Harry Potter at Hogwarts! Of course, my teachers aren't wizards, but they are very nice.

The staff wakes us up at 7 a.m. and we get ready for school. I take a shower and put on my uniform. We have breakfast in a large dining hall. There are lots of choices for breakfast. After breakfast, at 8:25 a.m., the teacher does the roll call to make sure everyone is present. Classes start at 9 a.m. and continue till 5:10 p.m. Monday to Thursday. On Fridays, they end at 4:35 p.m. There are two breaks in the day, and we have lunch from 1 p.m. till 2 p.m. I like Wednesdays because, after lunch, we have other activities—we play sports or music till 5:10 p.m. When school finishes, we usually walk to our rooms and get changed. Dinner is at 5:45 p.m. and prep starts at 7 p.m. Academic success is very important at my school. Prep finishes at 8:30 p.m. After that, we're free to relax and watch TV or chat with friends. Bedtime is at 10:15 p.m., although we have to be in our rooms by 10 p.m.

I miss my mom and dad some weekends, but in general life as a boarder is pretty good and I enjoy it. You meet lots of new people and make good friends.

My World

Reading > Away from Home

Getting the General Idea
Before you read a text in detail, skim it quickly to get a general idea of what it is about.

1 Skim the article and write the best title.
   a. Our Weekly Schedule
   b. The School Year
   c. The Life of a Boarder

2 Write the correct times next to the pictures.

3 Underline the correct options to complete the sentences.
   a. Sally goes to a boarding school because…
      1. academic success is important.
      2. she likes boarding school.
      3. her parents travel a lot.
   b. Day students…
      1. sleep at the school.
      2. sleep and eat at the school.
      3. go home when school finishes.
   c. Sally's favorite day is…
      1. Monday.
      2. Wednesday.
      3. Thursday.
   d. … is important for St. Margaret's Boarding School.
      1. Success in sports
      2. Free time
      3. Academic success
   e. Sally enjoys her school because…
      1. she goes home in the evening.
      2. she has lots of friends.
      3. the breakfast is very good.

Vocabulary > Telling the Time

1 Match the clocks to the times.

a. 03:00
b. 07:30
c. 04:15
d. 05:20

___ three o'clock
___ twenty past five/five twenty
___ a quarter past four/four fifteen
___ seven thirty

2 Write the times you do the following activities.
   Wake up: _____
   Have breakfast: _____
   Go to school: _____
   Do homework: _____
   Relax: _____
   Go to bed: _____

Listening > Comparing Schools

1 Listen to a man talking to his daughter and mark (✓) what they are comparing.
   a. Two schools in the US ___
   b. The girl's school to her friend's school ___
   c. The girl's school to a school in Canada ___

2 Listen again and mark the activities E (Emily) or M (Miguel).
   a. Goes to school at seven ___
   b. Wears a uniform ___
   c. Takes the school bus ___
   d. Buys lunch at school ___
   e. Doesn't have a locker ___

Grammar > Simple Present
(Affirmative and Negative)

1 Read the examples from *Track 9*. Underline the subjects and circle the verbs.

> I go to school at nine, but Miguel goes at seven.
> I don't wear special clothes, but he wears a uniform.
> His school has a cafeteria.
> We don't buy food.
> He doesn't have a locker at school, but we all have lockers at our school.
> Teachers give a lot of homework.
>
> See *Grammar Reference*, page 104.

2 Read the sentences again and mark the statements *T* (true) or *F* (false).

a. We use the simple present tense to describe facts and routines. ___

b. In the third person (he/she/it) affirmative sentences, the verb does not change. ___

c. We use *don't* and *doesn't* before the verb in negative sentences. ___

3 Write the third person singular forms of the verbs in the correct columns.

take   do   wear   work
watch   hurry   teach   fly

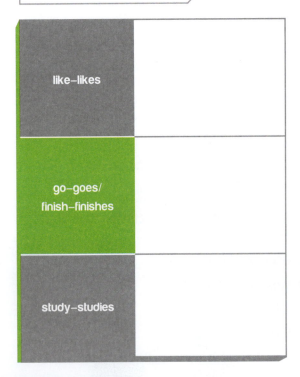

like–likes	
go–goes/ finish–finishes	
study–studies	

4 Look at the pictures and write about what Ashley and Sara do each day.

Speaking > Daily Routines

> Complete the first column with the times you do things. Then interview two classmates about their daily routines.

Get up			
Go to school			
Have lunch			
Finish school			
Get home			
Go to bed			

Views

Listening > Free Time

Listening for Specific Information
Before listening, identify the missing information. Then listen carefully for those details.

1. Look at the survey and identify the type of information it asks for.

2. Listen to teens Lisa and Jan discussing the survey. Say if Lisa is a lark or an owl.

3. Work in groups. Conduct a survey of your classmates to find out how many larks and owls there are in your class.

    Are you more active in the morning or the evening?

Pronunciation > /s/, /ɪz/, /z/

1. Listen and notice the pronunciation of the final -s.

/s/	/z/	/ɪz/
like – likes	live – lives	finish – finishes
eat – eats	go – goes	watch – watches

2. Write the third person forms of the verbs in the table according to their pronunciation.

    kiss   read   close   play   stop
    listen   visit   work   catch

3. Listen and check. Practice saying the words out loud.

TeenTimes Survey: Are you a lark or an owl?

We asked 412 young people what time of day they feel active. Here are the results:

- 60% day time
- 25% evening
- 15% morning people

What about you?

Take our free time survey and win a TeenTimes sweatshirt!

Age: _____

Gender: _____

1. What time do you get up and go to bed on Saturday?
    - Get up _____
    - Go to bed _____

2. What do you do on a typical Saturday? Write the activities next to the times of day.

    • Go online   • Listen to music   • Watch TV
    • Sleep   • Read a book   • Play sports   • Meet friends
    • Do homework   • Visit family   • Go shopping

    - In the morning: _____
    - In the afternoon: _____
    - In the evening: _____
    - At night: _____
    - Other (please specify): _____

3. Are you more active in the morning, afternoon, or evening?

Thank you! To participate in the raffle for the sweatshirt, write your e-mail address below.

Vocabulary > Leisure Activities

> Complete your typical weekend schedule with activities from the box. Add other activities as needed.

```
read a book      visit friends
go shopping      listen to music
      play video games
go to the movies    go to the park
   visit family    meet friends
   play sports     go to a party
```

Reading > Schools Connect

1 Skim the chat quickly and underline the best answers.

a. Who are Isa and Jesse?

1. Students from the same school.
2. Students from different schools.
3. Friends from the same town.

b. What are they chatting about?

1. Free time.
2. School.
3. Music and sports.

Weekend Schedule
September
19 Sat.
Morning   Afternoon   Evening
Night

20 Sun.
Morning   Afternoon   Evening
Night

Schoolsconnect.com

Schools active:
- Colegio Los Robles, Bogotá
- Forest Park High, Baltimore

Users: Isa ● Jesse

ISA: Hi Jesse! Are you busy?

JESSE: No, I'm not. Today I am not doing anything.

ISA: Do you normally go out on Fridays?

JESSE: Yes, I do. I go out with my friends. We go to the mall, but today it's too cold! Do you go out?

ISA: I watch TV or go on the computer.

JESSE: What about Saturdays? What do you do?

ISA: I do my homework in the morning. Then, in the afternoon, I go to my best friend's house. Her name's Debbie.

JESSE: Does she live close by?

ISA: No, she doesn't. She lives downtown.

JESSE: Is she the same age as you?

ISA: No, she isn't. She is one year older.

JESSE: I see. So what do you do on Sundays?

ISA: I visit my grandparents. They live in the suburbs. Do you visit your grandparents?

JESSE: No, I don't. They live in a different city.

2 Read the chat and write when Isa does each of the activities.

a. Does her homework _____

b. Watches TV or goes online _____

c. Goes to her best friend's house _____

d. Visits her grandparents _____

26 Unit 2

Grammar > Simple Present
(Questions and Short Answers)

1 Read the examples from the chat. Underline the auxiliary verbs and circle the main verbs.

> *Are you busy? No, I'm not.*
> *Do you go out on Fridays? Yes, I do.*
> *Does she live close by? No, she doesn't.*
> *Is she the same age as you? No, she isn't.*
> *What do you do on Sundays? I visit my grandparents.*
>
> See *Grammar Reference,* page 104.

2 Match the questions to the possible answers.

a. Do you read books? ____ Yes, she does./No, she doesn't.
b. Does she play basketball? ____ Yes, I am./No, I'm not.
c. What do you do on Fridays? ____ He goes by bus.
d. How does he go to school? ____ She paints.
e. Are you happy? ____ No, I don't./Yes, I do.
f. Is she happy? ____ No, she isn't./Yes, she is.
g. What is her hobby? ____ I relax./I don't go out.

3 Underline the correct options.

a. When *to be* is the *main/auxiliary* verb, we use it in short answers to questions.
b. We use the *main/auxiliary* verb in short answers to yes/no questions with the auxiliary verb *do*.
c. We use the *main/auxiliary* verb in answers to wh- questions with the auxiliary verb *do*.

4 Complete the dialogue with the correct form of the auxiliary *do* or the verb *to be*.

JEN: 1) _____ you like Saturdays?
MARK: Yes, I 2) _____.
JEN: What time 3) _____ you get up?
MARK: Late!
JEN: 4) _____ you always so lazy? Just kidding!
MARK: I 5) _____ not lazy! Very funny!
JEN: What 6) _____ you do in the afternoon?
MARK: I meet friends.
JEN: 7) _____ you visit your family on Saturdays?
MARK: No, I 8) _____. I see my best friend.
JEN: 9) _____ your best friend live close by?
MARK: No, he 10) _____. He lives in the suburbs.
JEN: 11) _____ he fun to hang out with?
MARK: Yes, he 12) _____!

Writing > Sister Schools

1 You are going to have an online chat with a student from a school in another country. Write a list of questions to ask.

2 Exchange questions with a classmate and write your answers to his or her questions.

SAM: Hi, Anna. Where do you live?
ANNA: Hi, Sam. I live in…

Out and About

Reading > **The Amish**

1. Look at the pictures and complete the predictions.
   a. The Amish *live/don't live* simple lives.
   b. Amish men *are/aren't* farmers.
   c. They *get up/don't get up* early.
   d. The Amish *use/don't use* electricity.
   e. They *drive/don't drive* cars.

2. Read the article and check your predictions.

3. Answers the questions.
   a. Where do Amish grandparents live?
   _____
   b. What do Amish children learn at school?
   _____
   c. Where do Amish children meet their friends?
   _____
   d. What do they use for light?
   _____

4. Write three differences between the lifestyles of Amish children and children in your country.

A Different Way of Life

Nowadays, many people live in big cities with lots of traffic, pollution, and noise. Not the Amish. They live very simple lives. Many Amish men are farmers, and women are usually homemakers.

Family is very important to the Amish. Grandparents normally live in the same house as children and grandchildren. Amish children have very different lives from most North American children. They get up early in the morning—around five o'clock—and make their beds, clean the house, or help with the farm animals. Then they go to school. They only go to school until the end of eighth grade. They learn to read and write, but they also learn how to grow plants, cook, and sew.

After school, Amish boys help their fathers in the fields every day, and girls work in the house or in the yard with their mothers.

Amish children don't go to public parks, movie theaters, or malls. They enjoy activities at home or on the farm. They meet their friends at school or once a week after church. Baseball is a popular sport among the Amish.

The Amish don't use electricity. They don't have radios, televisions, or computers. They use gas lamps for light and they usually travel by horse and buggy.

For most Amish people, preserving these old traditions is very important.

Vocabulary > Chores

1 Mark (✓) the chores you do.

make your bed
clean your room
buy groceries
clean the kitchen
help in the yard
set the table

2 Conduct a class survey. Find out what chores your classmates do.
Do you set the table? Yes, I do./No, I don't.

Writing > Helping Around the House

1 Write a weekly planner listing the chores you do around the house.

2 Work in groups. Compare your lists.

Listening > Tourists in Amish Communities

1 Tourists often visit Amish communities and ask questions about the local lifestyle. Write two questions you would ask.

2 Listen to a tourist and a local boy and check whether or not the visitor asks your questions.

3 Listen again and mark the statements *T* (true) or *F* (false).

   a. Jacob watches a lot of television. ___
   b. Jacob helps with the farm animals. ___
   c. He usually goes to school by horse and buggy. ___
   d. Jacob doesn't go to the movies. ___
   e. He goes into town three or four times a week. ___

4 Work in groups. Discuss the questions.

   a. Whhy is the tourist surprised?
   b. What things about Jacob's life are similar to yours?
   c. What things are different from your lifestyle?

Unit 2 29

Grammar > Adverbs of Frequency

1 Read the examples from *Track 13* and write the adverbs of frequency on the scale.

> I <u>always</u> get up early to help my dad with the animals.
> I <u>usually</u> walk to school. <u>Sometimes</u>, I go by horse and buggy.
> There's <u>often</u> a baseball game. They are usually three or four times a week.
> How often do you go into town? I <u>rarely</u> go into town. Maybe once or twice a month.
> I <u>never</u> go to the movies.

See *Grammar Reference*, page 105.

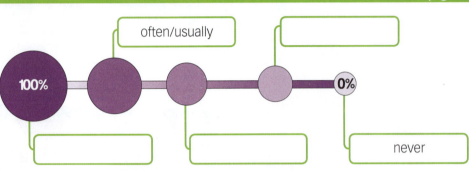

2 Answer the questions.

a. What question words do we use to ask about frequency?
_____

b. Do adverbs of frequency go before or after the verb *to be*?
_____

c. Do adverbs of frequency go before or after other verbs?
_____

3 In your notebook, write sentences saying how often your family members do the things in the pictures.

4 Unscramble the words and write the exchanges.

a. do / a / you / How often / movie / watch / ?
   watch / I / a / twice a week / movie / .
   _____
   _____

b. visit / Do / you / your / Saturdays / on / friends / often / ?
   I / Yes, / Saturdays / friends / visit / on / my / usually / .
   _____
   _____

c. do / have / your / How / lunch / often / grandparents / with / you / ?
   lunch / I / with / a / my / month / once / have / grandparents/ .
   _____
   _____

d. often / clean / you / room / your / do / How / ?
   my / once / I / room / week / a / clean / .
   _____
   _____

Speaking > How often...?

> Work in groups. Conduct a survey about how often your group members do each of the daily activities.

a. Get up before seven o'clock
b. Walk to school
c. Set the table at home
d. Eat lunch at school
e. Play sports
f. Do homework

Review

1. Write five sentences about your daily routine.

   I get up at 6:30.
   I have breakfast with my sister.

2. Look at the chore chart and write sentences about what each person does and doesn't do.

   Lily washes the dishes. She doesn't clean the kitchen.

   > Use the chore chart to write questions. Then work in pairs to ask and answer the questions.

   Do you buy the groceries?
   Yes, I do./No, I don't. My dad buys the groceries.

3. Look at Tony's weekly schedule and match the adverbs to the activities.

	Mon	Tues	Wed	Thurs	Fri
Get up	5:00	5:00	9:00	5:00	5:00
Watch TV	✗	✗	✗	✗	✗
Wash dishes	✓	✗	✓	✗	✓
Go to the movies	✗	✗	✗	✗	✓
Do exercise	✓	✓	✓	✓	✓

   a. always   ____ Get up early
   b. rarely   ____ Wash dishes
   c. never   ____ Watch TV
   d. sometimes   ____ Do exercise
   e. usually   ____ Go to the movies

   > Write sentences about Tony's weekly schedule.

   Tony usually gets up early.

4. Use the information in activity 3 to write questions with *how often*. Then work in pairs to ask and answer the questions.

   How often do you go to the movies on Saturdays?

5. Read the article and answer the questions.

   Fifteen year-old twins Monica and Greg don't meet friends on Saturdays like most teens. They have a business to run. They walk dogs. With around twenty canine customers, they get up very early. They eat breakfast and pick up the first dogs at 7 a.m. "We have to hurry. The dogs need to go outside, and the owners sometimes have to work," says Monica. "We always go to the park first. We usually play games and run around with the dogs." The twins offer walks at any time, depending on the owner's schedule. The key to their success? "We love animals and we are never late!"

   a. Why are Monica and Greg different from most teens?
   b. What do they do on the walks?
   c. Why is punctuality important for their business?

Unit 2   31

3 My Favorites

Value Sharing Sharing can make the world a better place

1 Mark (✓) what you share with friends.
   - ☐ clothes
   - ☐ computer
   - ☐ money
   - ☐ phone
   - ☐ snacks
   - ☐ books

2 Work in pairs. Compare your answers and discuss the questions.
   a. Do you share the same things?
   b. What other things do you share?
   c. What else do you not share?

What's your favorite subject?

In a recent survey of students in the US aged 13 to 17, 23% of students say math is their favorite subject. The pie chart shows other popular subjects.

Another survey shows that boys and girls have different opinions about some subjects, but 8% of students say they don't have a favorite subject at school.

Students like subjects for different reasons. Here are some:

"My favorite subject is math because there are clear right and wrong answers."
— Sarah, 14

"My favorite is science because it is logical."
— John, 15

"I like English because it is creative."
— Andy, 17

"I like math because my teacher explains problems really well."
— Sam, 16

But not all students give academic reasons. One teen says:

"I like study hall and P.E. In study hall I do my homework, and in P.E. I exercise. They are my favorite subjects!"
— Max, 13

What about you? Do you have a favorite subject?

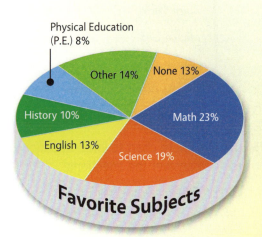

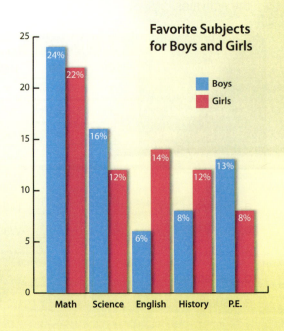

My World

Reading > Favorite Subjects

Anticipating Content
Read the title and think about the topic. This helps you to understand the text.

1 Underline the statement you think is true.
   a. Boys and girls like different school subjects.
   b. Boys and girls like the same school subjects.

2 Read the article. Mark the sentences T (true) or F (false).
   a. The survey is about schools. ___
   b. Twelve percent of girls in a survey say math is their favorite subject. ___
   c. English is the favorite subject of 6% of boys. ___
   d. Most girls like P.E. ___
   e. Not all students have a favorite subject. ___
   f. One student likes P.E. because he can be creative. ___

3 Complete the sentences.
   a. The students in the survey are _____ years old.
   b. There are clear right and wrong answers in _____.
   c. One student likes science because it is _____.
   d. One student likes English because it is _____.
   e. You can do homework in _____.

Vocabulary > School Subjects

> Mark (✓) the subjects you study.

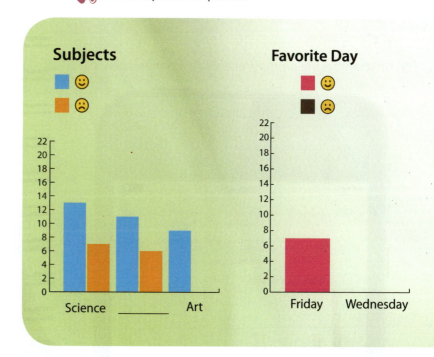

Listening > Likes and Dislikes at School

1 Complete the missing words in the survey questions.
   a. What is your favorite _____? Science.
   b. What is your favorite _____? Friday.
   c. Who is your favorite _____? Miss Johnson.

2 Listen and complete the poster.

3 Listen again and underline the correct information.
   a. Ana *loves/hates* science.
   b. Tom loves *math/art*.
   c. Miss *Johnson/Robinson* is their favorite teacher.
   d. Ana doesn't like *Wednesdays/Fridays*.
   e. Tom *loves/hates* Wednesdays.

Unit 3   33

Grammar > Expressing Likes and Dislikes

1 Read the extracts and underline the verbs. Draw the icons.

I hate science. ___
You don't like math. ___
We like art. ___
They love drama. ___

See *Grammar Reference*, page 105.

2 Complete the table with the words from the sentences in activity 1.

Subject	Verb	Object
I	hate	math
You	like	art
		drama

> Form new sentences and write them in your notebook.

3 Unscramble the prompts and write the messages.

a. Saturdays! / I / 😀
   I love Saturdays!

b. 😞 / we / π
   _____

c. they / Mondays / 😖
   _____

d. Miss Johnson / we / 🙂
   _____

Speaking > A Class Survey

1 Work in groups. Prepare survey questions to ask about the following topics.
   • Subject
   • Day
   • Teacher

2 Work with another group. Make the survey and take notes.

3 Present the information to the class.

Useful Language

*Five people love… and
three people don't like…
Seven people hate…
One person likes… but…*

34 Unit 3

Views

Listening ▸ Teenager Likes and Dislikes

Listening for Confirmation
When we listen, some information is new and some information we already know. Information we know helps us to understand new information better.

1 Work in pairs. Look at the forum and discuss what it is about.

2 Listen 🎧 and complete the forum profiles.

3 Listen again and mark the likes (✓) and dislikes (✗).

	Kim	Dan
shopping		
video games		
Miley Cyrus		

Pronunciation ▸ /ɪ/ vs /iː/

1 Look at the underlined sounds. Then listen 🎧 and classify the words.

| s<u>ea</u>t   s<u>i</u>t   <u>ea</u>t   h<u>e</u>'s   h<u>i</u>s   <u>i</u>t |

/ɪ/ sit, _____, _____

/iː/ seat, _____, _____

2 Listen 🎧 to the sentences and underline the words you hear.

a. *sit/seat*   c. *he's/his*   e. *it/eat*
b. *sit/seat*   d. *he's/his*   f. *it/eat*

> Work in pairs. Practice saying the words in sentences.

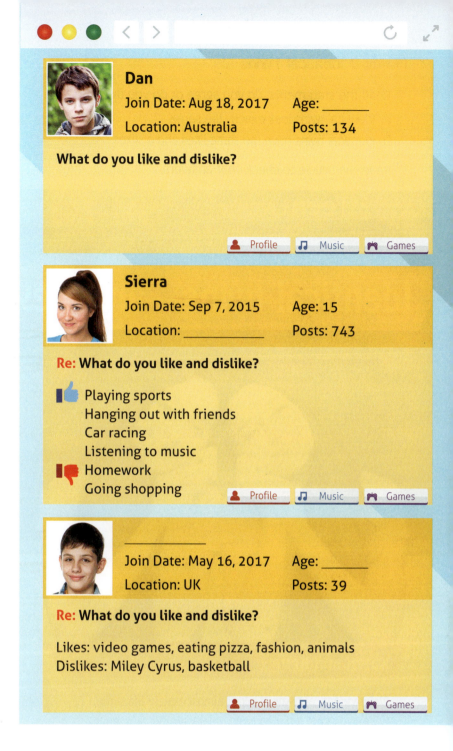

Dan
Join Date: Aug 18, 2017   Age: _____
Location: Australia   Posts: 134

What do you like and dislike?

Profile | Music | Games

Sierra
Join Date: Sep 7, 2015   Age: 15
Location: _____   Posts: 743

Re: What do you like and dislike?

👍 Playing sports
   Hanging out with friends
   Car racing
   Listening to music
👎 Homework
   Going shopping

Profile | Music | Games

_____
Join Date: May 16, 2017   Age: _____
Location: UK   Posts: 39

Re: What do you like and dislike?

Likes: video games, eating pizza, fashion, animals
Dislikes: Miley Cyrus, basketball

Profile | Music | Games

Writing ▸ A Great Weekend

1 Write the activities in the table.

| chatting online   hanging out with friends   listening to music |
| playing guitar   playing video games   reading books |

Individual	Group or Pair	Both

2 Make a list of five activities you like doing on the weekend.

Unit 3   35

Reading > Identical Twins

1 Read the statements: do you agree or do you disagree?
   a. Identical twins look exactly the same.
   b. Identical twins have the same likes and dislikes.

2 Read the article to check your answers.

Teen Lives

Identical twins—are they really identical?

Karen and Keira

We are identical twins. We look almost exactly the same, but we are very different in the things we like and don't like. I like reading books, but Karen likes playing video games. I like chatting online, but she likes hanging out with friends. She loves playing volleyball, but I hate it! We have one thing in common, we love our dog but we both hate walking it. It likes sleeping a lot—similar to Karen!

Billy and Ben

People always confuse us. We like the same clothes. We like going shopping and hanging out with friends. We both love listening to music. But there is one big difference. Ben likes rap and I like rock music. He doesn't like rock and I hate rap! I love playing guitar and bass guitar. Ben doesn't play musical instruments, but he likes singing.

3 Read the text again and underline the correct options.
   a. Karen and Keira are identical *friends/cousins/twins*.
   b. Karen likes *chatting online/hanging out with friends/dogs*.
   c. Keira hates *playing video games/walking their dog/sleeping*.
   d. Billy and Ben like the same *clothes/people/shops*.
   e. Billy *likes/doesn't like/hates* rap.
   f. Ben likes *playing bass guitar/singing/reading books*.

Grammar > **Expressing Likes and Dislikes**
(Third Person Singular)

1 Read the extracts and underline the verbs.

> *Karen likes playing video games.*
> *She loves playing volleyball.*
> *Ben likes rap.*
> *He doesn't like rock.*
> *It likes sleeping.*

See *Grammar Reference,* page 105.

2 Complete the rules.
   a. After *he, she,* or *it*, we add _____ to the verb.
   b. In negative sentences, we use _____ before the verb without -s.

3 Complete the article with the information in parentheses.

4 Work in pairs. Cover the article and say what you remember about the twins.

Writing > **Describing Likes and Dislikes**

1 Write a list of activities you and your best friend love, like, don't like, and hate.

	Me	
love		
like		
don't like		
hate		

2 Write a short article for *Teen Lives* about you and your friend.

My best friend and I are very similar. We love…

Li Jing and Zhang Li

Teen Lives

We look the same, exactly the same! And we both love hanging out with friends, we are social! We also like sports. I 1) _____ (☺/play football) and Zhang Li 2) _____ (☺/play basketball). We both 3) _____ (☹/play video games), we like to be active. There is one important difference, I 4) _____ (☺/ go shopping) and fashion, but Zhang Li 5) _____ (☹) that. She 6) _____ (☺/listen to music) and playing guitar. I 7) _____ (☺/ play drums) at school, but Zhang Li 8) _____ (☹) it.

Unit 3 37

Out and About

Reading > Fashion in Brazil

1. Look at the article pictures and underline the best title.

   a. Fashion Everywhere
   b. I Hate My Clothes
   c. Different People, Different Clothes

2. Read the article and circle the names of the clothes.

3. Complete the table.

Clothes in Brazil	Why
jeans, cowboy hats, cowboy boots	
	They are traditional.
loose pants, belt	
T-shirts, shorts, sandals, swimsuits	
	People wear them to work.
jeans, T-shirts, sneakers	

Vocabulary > Clothes

1. Circle the clothes in the article pictures.

   boots   dress   hat   jeans   pants
   necklace   shorts   sneakers   belt   T-shirt

2. Complete the sentences.

   a. At school, I wear _____ .

   b. At home, I wear _____ .

   c. When I go out with my friends, I wear _____ .

People in Brazil like fashion, and clothes are important to them. Many Brazilians love bright colors and fashionable styles, but their clothes are different in different parts of the country. The northern style isn't similar to the style in southern Brazil, for example.

In the south of the country the majority of people work on ranches. They wear jeans, cowboy hats, and cowboy boots.

There is a strong African influence in Bahia, in the north of Brazil. Women often wear beautiful traditional dresses. People from the Amazon region often wear beads and body paint. Capoeira dancers wear loose pants with a belt—their clothes are very comfortable.

Rio de Janeiro is famous for its beaches, and people there often wear T-shirts, shorts and sandals, or swimsuits! São Paulo is the business center of the country and people there often go to work in suits.

Brazil is a unique country, but in one way it is similar to other countries in the world. The favorite casual clothes for most people are jeans, T-shirts, and sneakers.

38   Unit 3

Writing > Giving an Opinion

1 Read and underline the correct clothes.

> ▶ 1 COMMENT
>
> **TIM FORD**
> September 5, 2017 at 4:00 p.m.
>
> I like the cowboy pants/dress. They look comfortable. I like the hat/T-shirt too, but I don't like the pants/boots. I hate the color. I think the boots are horrible!
>
> **SUBMIT**

2 Write a comment about the clothes of someone in the article.

Listening > Fashion Week

1 Look at the poster and say which clothes you like.

2 Listen 🎧 to a conversation and circle in the poster the clothes you hear.

3 Listen again and mark the the statements T (true) or F (false).

   a. She likes the man's pants. ___
   b. He likes the man's pants. ___
   c. He likes the man's boots. ___
   d. She doesn't like the jackets. ___
   e. He likes the jackets. ___

Unit 3   39

Grammar > Possessive Adjectives

1 Read the extracts and underline the possessive adjectives.

> I love his pants.
> Your boots are black.
> My boots are black.
> I like their jackets.
> Her necklace is great.
> Our clothes are always fantastic.
>
> See *Grammar Reference*, page 105.

2 Write the possessive adjectives beside the pronouns.

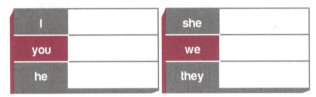

3 Underline the correct option to complete the rule.

Possessive adjectives go *before/after* the noun.

4 Underline the correct possessive adjectives in the messages.

5 Complete the rest of the chat.

Speaking > Spot the Differences

> Work in pairs.
> Student A: Turn to page 92.
> Student B: Turn to page 94.

40 Unit 3

Review

1 Circle ten pieces of clothing in the word square.

D	V	D	R	E	S	S	L	N	T
G	B	O	O	T	S	V	B	A	S
W	M	R	A	O	C	P	H	S	H
S	N	E	A	K	E	R	S	H	I
J	N	A	C	K	H	U	G	O	R
E	H	L	B	K	A	M	O	R	T
A	Y	F	E	F	T	F	S	T	Y
N	R	X	L	P	L	O	W	S	T
S	W	O	T	Y	P	A	N	T	S
N	E	C	K	L	A	C	E	S	F

2 Look at the graphs and describe the results in your notebook.

Four students love history.

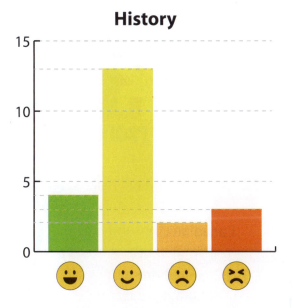

3 Look at the table and describe Ana's and Tom's likes and dislikes.

	Ana	Tom	Me
chatting online	😖	😖	
going shopping	😕	🙂	
reading books	🙂	😕	

_____
_____
_____

4 Complete the table above with your information.

5 Complete the description with the correct words.

Fashionista Teen

 Meet My New Friends
Friday, October 11th 2017, 2:30 p.m.

These are 1) _____ new friends Matt and Arlene. Matt loves music. 2) _____ favorite possession is an electric guitar he carries everywhere. Arlene likes movies. 3) _____ favorite actress is Jennifer Lawrence. Fashion isn't important for Matt and Arlene! They like jeans, sneakers, and T-shirts, like me! 4) _____ clothes are very similar, we have the same style!

6 Read the article and answer the questions.

A Different Type of Friend

Sharing time with friends is very important. *Big Brothers, Big Sisters* is a program that helps young people with problems have a better future. The program matches *Bigs* (mentors) with *Littles* (young people) based on location, personalities, and preferences. They don't need a special occasion or an expensive activity to share time. They do activities they enjoy, like playing sports, reading, going to a museum, or just hanging out together. It's a win-win situation!

a. What does the *Big Brothers, Big Sisters* program do?
b. What do *Bigs* and *Littles* do together?
c. What do *Bigs* help to improve?

Unit 3   41

4 Something Special

Value Appreciation For your life to be great, first learn to appreciate it! 4A

1 Write something or someone that is special for you in each category.

A possession _____

A person _____

A place _____

2 Compare what you wrote with another student. Say which of the things is the most important to you.

My World

Reading > Skateboarding

Making Connections
When reading, think about the topic in relation to people and things in your life. Good readers associate what they read with the world around them.

1 Look at the pictures and answer the questions.
   a. What are the people doing?
   b. What do you know about this sport?

2 Read the skateboarders' profiles to check.

The Flip

The Slide

The Grind

SK-8-ERS PROFILES

NAME: Keysha
AGE: 14
NATIONALITY: Canadian (Toronto)

Skateboarding is a great sport. You can practice it anywhere around the city. All you need is a skateboard and a bit of equipment. I always skate after school and on the weekends. I just want to have fun. There's a great skateboard park near me. I go with my friends. My board is really special. It's a long board with a custom design. I love bright colours. My inspiration is Leticia Bufoni. She is from São Paulo. Her tricks are brilliant—her slides and flips are out of this world. I want to be like her one day.

3 Mark the sentences T (true) or F (false).

   a. Keysha doesn't usually skate after school. ___
   b. She skates alone. ___
   c. She uses a long skateboard. ___
   d. Tyson and Claudia think it's important to wear helmets and pads. ___
   e. They practice on the streets. ___
   f. Claudia doesn't like SK-8-ERS magazine. ___

4 Answer the questions in your notebook.
   a. Why do you think skateboarders like personalising their skateboards?
   b. Why is it important to wear hats and pads?
   c. Do you think it is OK for skateboarders to practice in public places like parks?

SK-8-ERS PROFILES

NAMES: Tyson and Claudia
AGES: 15 and 16
NATIONALITY: Brazilian (Rio de Janeiro)

Claudia and I spend a lot of free time practicing our tricks. Some of them are really dangerous. It's really important when you skateboard to have the right equipment. We always wear helmets, pads, and gloves. The type of board is really important too. We have a lot of different boards. There are a lot of really good designs. Rob Berstein is a great skater and someone whose boards are really beautiful. My favorite board is pure black and Claudia has a picture of Copacabana beach. It's a great sport for the city. We practice in skate parks. I love doing flips and grinds on the ramp. We both read SK-8-ERS—it's a great magazine!

Vocabulary > **Skateboarding**

> Write words from the text.

Things You Need to Skateboard

s _ _ _ _ _ _ _ _ _ _ (10 letters)

p _ _ _ _ (4 letters)

h _ _ _ _ _ _ (6 letters)

Things You Do on a Skateboard

t _ _ _ _ _ _ (6 letters)

f _ _ _ _ (4 letters)

g _ _ _ _ _ (5 letters)

Listening > **Expressing Preferences**

1 Look at the skateboards. Tell other students which you prefer.

2 Listen and circle the board the speakers prefer.

3 Listen again and match the skateboards to the owners.

Lily ___   Julie ___   Terry ___

Matt ___   Emma ___

Unit 4   43

Grammar > **Whose and Possessive Pronouns**

1 Read the extracts from *Track 19* and underline the correct options.

> *Whose is this board? Is it yours?*
> *No, it's Terry's. Mine is black.*
> *Is this one Julie's?*
> *No, hers has a picture of Rio.*
> *Whose board is it?*
> *It isn't Matt's. His is red and white.*
> *Here come Jade and Marcy. Maybe it's theirs.*
> *No, it isn't ours.*
>
> See *Grammar Reference*, page 106.

a. We use *whose* to ask about *time/possession*.
b. We use the underlined words to refer to *the person(s)/the person's(s') possession*.

2 Complete the table with the underlined words.

Personal pronoun	Possessive pronoun
I	
you	yours
he	
she	
we	
they	

3 Answer the questions. Use a possessive pronoun.

Whose is this pen? (It's your pen.)

  It's mine!

a. Whose is this board? (It's Susanna's.)
  _____

b. Whose pads are these? (They're Rory's.)
  _____

c. Whose are these helmets? (They're Andrea's and Jo's.) _____

d. Whose board is this? (It's your board.)
  _____

e. Whose trainers are these? (They're you and your friends'.) _____

4 Match the people to the objects.

5 Write questions and answers about the pictures above.

a. Whose are these shoes?
  _____

b. _____
  _____

c. _____
  _____

44 Unit 4

Views

Listening > **A Special Present**

Listening for Emotions
Speakers often express emotion by emphasizing certain words and using intonation. As you listen, try to identify the emotion the speaker is feeling.

1 Listen to the conversations and connect the people to the places. There is one extra place.

a. Melinda ___ at home
b. Roy ___ in a toy shop
c. Brenda, Will, and Dad ___ at school
___ at a football stadium

2 Listen again and underline the correct answers.

a. Grace suggests buying Gary…
 1) football boots.
 2) a football.
 3) a football video game.
b. Melinda decides to get…
 1) a football.
 2) a football shirt.
 3) a ticket to a football game.
c. Roy wants to give Susan chocolates because…
 1) she is feeling sad.
 2) it is a joke.
 3) he really likes her.
d. The problem is that…
 1) Susan doesn't like chocolates.
 2) Susan isn't coming to school today.
 3) he is putting the chocolates in the wrong desk.
e. For his birthday, Brenda and Will give their dad…
 1) a video game.
 2) a book.
 3) a photo album.
f. The problem is that…
 1) he can't change it.
 2) he has it.
 3) he doesn't like the present.

Pronunciation > **Expressing Emotions**

1 Listen and match the extracts to how the speakers feel.

a. Melinda ___ surprised
b. Roy ___ disappointed
c. Will ___ enthusiastic

2 Listen again and underline the words the speakers emphasize.

a. GRACE: Why don't you buy him tickets for next week's game?
 MELINDA: Hey, that's a great idea! I love it!
b. CARRIE: That's a really nice idea but that's not Susan's desk!
 ROY: Really?
c. DAD: It's a video game. It's a great game but I have this one.
 WILL: Oh no!

Vocabulary > **Ordinals 20th-100th**

1 Match the ordinals to the cards.

twenty-first   twenty-sixth   fiftieth
seventieth   ninetieth

2 Listen and say.
23rd   34th   47th   56th   62nd   71st   89th

Reading > What's up?

1 Work in groups. Discuss the questions.
   a. How many text messages do you send each day?
   b. Do you use emojis?

2 Read the messages and circle what the teens are texting about.

   | homework   a sports event   a present for a friend   gossip |

3 Match the emojis to a feeling.

   | happy   sad   funny   jealous   surprised   nervous |

Unit 4

Grammar > *What/How about* + Noun or Gerund

1 Read the extracts and label them *S* (suggestion), *PR* (positive response), *NR* (negative response).

> *What about a T-shirt?* ___
> *I don't know his size.* ___
> *How about giving him a gift voucher?* ___
> *Cool!* ___
>
> See *Grammar Reference*, page 106.

2 Complete the rules.

> noun   How   -ing

a. We make suggestions with the expressions *What about…?* and _____ *about…?*

b. We follow the expressions with a _____ or the _____ form of a verb.

3 Match the responses to the suggestions.

a. How about going to the movies?

b. I'm thirsty. What about getting a drink?

c. What about some spaghetti for dinner?

d. I'm bored. What about a game of cards?

___ Sure! What games do you know?
___ I can't. I have a lot of homework.
___ No, I don't like spaghetti.
___ Good idea! I'm thirsty too.

4 Unscramble the dialogues.

a. about / How / popcorn / some / buying / ?
_____

a / idea / great / That's / !
_____

b. taking / What / photos / about / some / ?
_____

can't. / I / battery's / dead. / My
_____

c. hot / It's / today. / about / What / ice cream / an / ?
_____

d. idea / Good / !
_____

Writing > A Friendly Chat

> Write the conversation. Include emojis.

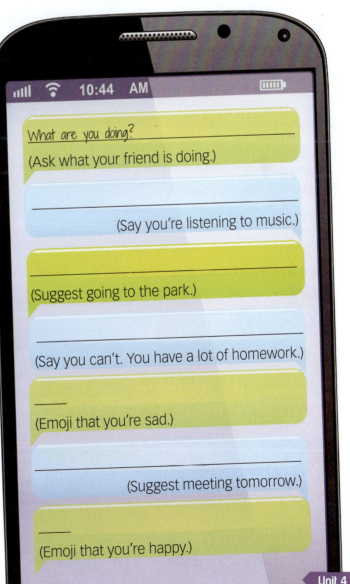

Unit 4   47

Out and About

Reading > Top Three

1 Read the text and label the places.

My Top Three Special Places
by our travel writer Karen Swales

1st Pico da Neblina is a mysterious mountain in a remote part of the Amazon rainforest. It is difficult to see it because it rains a lot there and thick clouds usually cover the mountain. Many unique species of plants and animals live there.

Indigenous Yanomami people live in the area. They believe that spirits live in caves near there. For the Yanomami, the caves are sacred and they do not usually permit visitors to go there.

2nd Lagoinha is a beautiful beach in the northeast of Brazil. It takes about half an hour to get to Lagoinha from the town of Paraipaba. The beach is very quiet during the week but it is busy on the weekends. The beach is popular with local young people. They go there to surf and hang out. A local legend says that there is a valuable French pirate treasure buried near the beach.

3rd Valparaíso is a city on the Pacific Coast of Chile. People often call it "The Jewel of the Pacific." The city is famous for its picturesque historic districts. Thousands of tourists visit every year to walk along the old streets and take pictures of the colorful houses.

The historic districts have an interesting and lively street life. They are full of musicians and street artists and there are also many typical cafés. From the top of the historic districts there is a wonderful view of the coast and the port.

2 Read again and mark the sentences *T* (true) or *F* (false).

a. It rains a lot on the Pico da Neblina. ___

b. A lot of visitors go to the caves near there. ___

c. The beach at Lagoinha is always busy. ___

d. There is Spanish treasure buried near the beach. ___

e. Valparaíso is an old city. ___

f. You can see the sea from Valparaíso. ___

3 Find reasons in the text for these things.

a. Why people don't visit the caves

_____

_____

b. Why the beach is busy at the weekends

_____

_____

c. Why tourists visit Valparaíso

_____

_____

48 Unit 4

Vocabulary > Describing Special Places

1 Write the adjectives from the text beside the correct definitions.

> mysterious   sacred   beautiful
> quiet   popular   colorful

a. without noise; tranquil _____

b. something that deserves respect and reverence
_____

c. unusual or strange _____

d. with a lot of color _____

e. very attractive _____

f. something many people like or enjoy
_____

2 Name the things in the text these adjectives describe.

> lively   historic   typical

Writing > Special Places

> Write sentences about a place that is special for you. Use adjectives from the text.
Street life in Rio is very lively!

Listening > Directions

1 Work in pairs. Say which of the places you would like to go to.

the forest

the beach

the mall

the park

2 Listen and number the places in the order the people mention them. There is one extra place.

3 Listen again and write the numbers of the places.

a. The road isn't very good. ___

b. Go through the gate. ___

c. I don't want to take all day. ___

d. The bus takes a long time. ___

e. About ten minutes. ___

f. From here to there takes hours. ___

Grammar > *How long does it take?*

1 Read the examples and answer the questions.

> *How long does it take?*
> *Not long. About ten minutes.*
> *How long does it take to walk to the park?*
> *It takes a long time.*
>
> See *Grammar Reference,* page 106.

a. What do the speakers ask about—time or distance?
_____

b. What question words do they use?
_____

c. What verb do they use?
_____

2 Look at the information and complete the conversation.

Travel information
Grantville to Springfield

	Dep	Arr
🚌	8:00	8:40
🚇	8:10	8:25
🚲	2 hours approx	
🚶	4 hours approx	

A: Excuse me. How long does it take to go from Grantville to Springfield by train?
B: It takes 1) _____ minutes.
A: How long does it take to 2) _____?
B: It takes about four hours.
A: How long does it 3) _____ to go by bus?
B: It takes 4) _____ minutes.
A: How long does it take to cycle?
B: It takes about 5) _____ hours.

3 Write a conversation from the prompts.

Excuse me… how long / take / walk to the beach?
Excuse me… How long does it take to walk to the beach?

To the beach? It / take / a long time
_____

Oh no! / I / not want / take all day
_____

take / bus
_____

How long / take?
_____

It / take / about half an hour.
_____

Speaking > Finding Travel Information

> Work in pairs. Find travel information.
> Student A: Turn to page 92.
> Student B: Turn to page 94.

Review

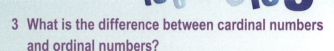

1 Underline your answers to the quiz.

1 Which is an example of an ordinal number?
   a. one
   b. twenty-two
   c. thirtieth
   d. five percent

2 What ordinal number corresponds to the cardinal number 45?
   a. Both forty-fifth and 45th
   b. 450th
   c. 45th only
   d. Forty-fifth only

3 What is the difference between cardinal numbers and ordinal numbers?
   a. Cardinal numbers tell us how many items there are. Ordinal numbers tell us the position of the items in a sequence.
   b. Ordinal numbers tell us how many items there are. Cardinal numbers tell us the position of the items in a sequence.

2 Rewrite the sentences with possessive pronouns.

a. That's my pen. It's _____.

b. John has a red board and this one is green.
   It isn't _____.

c. Our helmets are better than Jane's. _____ are better than _____.

d. Terry and John have black skateboards.
   _____ are the same color.

3 Complete the dialogue with the missing words.

| red   skateboard   a helmet |
| blue   buying |

Oscar: What about 1) _____ John
   2) _____?

Tamara: He has a helmet. How about a new
   3) _____?

Oscar: Good idea. What color?

Tamara: What about 4) _____?

Oscar: He doesn't like blue. How about
   5) _____?

Tamara: Fantastic!

4 Match the texts to the cartoons.
   a. How long does it take to fly to New York?
      It takes about five hours.
   b. How long does it take to get to Mars?
      A long time!

5 Ask and answer how long it takes to get from school to these places.
   • your friend's house
   • the train station
   • the main park

Unit 4   51

5 Animal Antics

Value Compassion Compassion for animals is a sign of our humanity

1. Work in groups. Discuss ways to help animals in your community.
2. Share your group's ideas with the class. Vote on the three best ideas.

Q&A

Food/Health

Choosing a Pet

Pets' Corner

▶ Which is the right pet for you?

The United States is a nation of pet lovers. Over 69 million homes have pets, including 73 million dogs and 90 million cats. A Department of Health study showed that keeping a pet is good for people's health. Still, owning a pet is a lot of responsibility. The Humane Society of the United States takes in thousands of abandoned animals each year. If you are ready to commit to taking care of a pet, it is important to choose the right one for your lifestyle.

Dogs and cats are the most popular pets. Dogs are a great idea for people who have time to spend with their pets. They need exercise and regular walks, so they are good for people who have a yard or live in rural areas. Dogs love running around outside, wagging their tails, chasing a ball, and playing with other dogs.

Dogs are not for everyone, though. Some breeds lose a lot of hair. This can be bad news for people with allergies. Dogs also need a lot of attention, especially young and small dogs. They often bark loudly or dig holes in the yard when they are bored. Dogs need a lot of training to stay out of trouble. Many people decide having one is too much work.

Cats require less work than dogs. They are usually very clean. They are quiet and independent too. People who live in small apartments may prefer owning a cat. Some cats like playing with their owners, but, unlike dogs, cats are also comfortable being alone.

However, cats sometimes jump onto chairs and tables and scratch things, including your best furniture! Some cats like climbing trees – the problem is that they can't always get down again. Also, most cats lose a lot of hair, so they aren't the best choice for people with allergies.

If you are ready to commit to owning a dog or cat, consider adopting one in need of a home. Your local animal shelter is a good place to start.

My World

Reading > **Ideal Pets**

Scanning for Specific Information
When reading to find specific information about a topic, ask yourself what information you want to find. Then read the text quickly to find it.

1 Answer the questions.
  a. Which pets are best for people who like being outdoors?
  b. Which pets are best for busy people who do not have much time?
  c. Which pets are best for people who do not have a lot of space?

2 Scan the website to see if the writer agrees with you.

3 Read the website and mark the phrases C (cats) or D (dogs).
  a. Need lots of exercise ___
  b. Are very clean ___
  c. Are happy to be alone ___
  d. Get bored easily ___
  e. Scratch things ___
  f. Are independent ___

4 Answer the questions.
  a. What care do fish and birds require?
  b. How are cats and dogs most different?
  c. Why do you think owning a pet improves people's health?
  d. Is it better to adopt a pet or buy one from a pet store? Why?

Vocabulary > **Action Verbs**

1 Decide which pets do the activities.

cat dog goldfish parrot

  a. dig   h. wag
  b. run   i. swim
  c. chase   j. sleep
  d. jump   k. climb
  e. walk   l. fly
  f. sit   m. chat
  g. bark   n. scratch

2 Complete the text with the correct form of verbs from activity 1.

My dog is named Arthur. When I arrive home, he 1) _____ loudly and 2) _____ his tail. I take him to the park and we play. I throw a ball into the air and he 3) _____ up and catches it. Then he 4) _____ around the park and 5) _____ the birds. Sometimes he 6) _____ a hole. When we get home, he 7) _____ for an hour because all the playing makes him tired.

Listening > **Unusual Pets**

1 Work in pairs. Discuss whether or not the animals in the pictures make good or bad pets.

2 Listen to two friends discuss unusual pets. Write answers to the questions.
  a. What is the boy's pet? _____
  b. What pets does the girl want? _____

3 Listen again and write the names of the animals described.
  a. Hides in cage: _____
  b. Talks a lot: _____
  c. Eats flies: _____
  d. Expensive to feed: _____

Unit 5 53

Grammar > Gerunds (-ing)

1 Read the examples from *Track 24* and underline the gerunds (-*ing* form).

> I don't like cleaning his cage.
> He loves climbing up my arm.
> How about getting an iguana?
> He enjoys hiding in his cage.
> Feeding him is the easy part—he only eats flies!
>
> See *Grammar Reference,* page 106.

2 Underline the correct option to complete the sentences.

a. We use gerunds to describe *activities/routines*.

b. We can use verbs such as *like*, *love,* and *enjoy* with the *gerund/base form* to express preferences.

c. We can use *let's* and *how about* to *express preferences/make suggestions*.

d. We follow *let's* with the *gerund/base form* of a verb and *how about* with the *gerund/base form*.

3 Refer to the examples in activity 1 and write the gerund forms of the verbs in the table.

| swim | live | run | dig | chase |
| ride | ~~eat~~ | buy | play | |

Verb + -*ing*	Drop final *e* and add -*ing*	Double the final consonant and add -*ing*
eat-eating		

4 Complete the sentences with the gerunds from activity 3.

a. The neighbor's dog loves _____ holes in our yard. My mom hates it!

b. My cat doesn't like _____ in the car.

c. My rabbit likes _____ oats. It's an herbivore.

d. I don't like _____ with my dog. He is too fast for me!

e. How about _____ a game?

f. My dog doesn't like _____. He hates water.

Speaking > A New Pet

1 Work in pairs to choose a new pet. Use the pictures and the prompts to write a conversation.

A: Suggest a pet.

B: Say no and give a reason. Suggest a different pet.

A: Say no and give a reason. Suggest another pet.

B: Say no and give a reason.

A: Agree/Disagree and make another suggestion.

B: Agree with the suggestion.

2 Practice the conversation aloud. Act it out for the class.

Views

Listening ▸ **Urban Wildlife**

> **Listening for Specific Information**
> When listening to a longer conversation, concentrate on key words. Do not try to understand every word.

1 Listen 🎧 to a radio program about wildlife in cities. Mark (✓) the animals the speakers mention.

2 Listen again and write the animal that lives in each place.

   a. drain: _____
   b. attic: _____
   c. trees: _____
   d. yard: _____

3 Underline the correct answers.

   a. Why do animals like living in cities?
      1. To be with people.
      2. To find food.
      3. To escape from danger.

   b. How do bats locate small insects?
      1. With their eyes.
      2. With radar.
      3. With their noses.

   c. How does the speaker describe rats?
      1. Dangerous.
      2. Agile.
      3. Terrible.

   d. Why are monkeys terrible neighbors?
      1. They live in trees.
      2. They chase cats and dogs.
      3. They invade people's houses.

   e. Where is there a legend about crocodiles in the drains?
      1. London.
      2. Nevada.
      3. New York.

○ bat ○ fly ○ rat ○ monkey ○ bird ○ fox ○ bear ○ elephant ○ crocodile ○ lion

Pronunciation ▸ **Syllable Stress**

1 Listen 🎧 and underline the stressed syllable in each word.

   today   different   people
   distance   recent   legend

2 Listen again and notice the pronunciation of the unstressed syllables. Practice saying the words aloud.

3 Mark the stressed syllable in each word.

   table   travel   arrive   normal   collect
   woman   parents   famous   attack

4 Practice saying the words aloud. Then listen 🎧 and check.

Unit 5   55

Vocabulary > Animals

> Match the animals to the descriptions.

a. bat
b. crocodile
c. bear
d. monkey
e. fox
f. rat

____ A small agile animal that lives in tunnels and drains.
____ Usually lives in the woods and eats fruit and fish.
____ A large reptile that lives in rivers.
____ An intelligent animal that lives in trees.
____ Sometimes makes its den in people's yards.
____ Normally lives in caves in the wild.

Reading > Urban Animal Profiles

1 Mark the sentences *T* (true) or *F* (false).

a. The red fox lives for 10 years. ____
b. They only eat meat. ____
c. They are good hunters. ____
d. They enjoy playing with people. ____

2 Read the profile and check your answers.

3 In your notebook, write answers to the questions.

a. What are red foxes famous for?
b. What do they do when they find a small animal?
c. What do they use their eyes and ears for?
d. What do they do before they attack the animal?
e. Why do they visit people's yards?

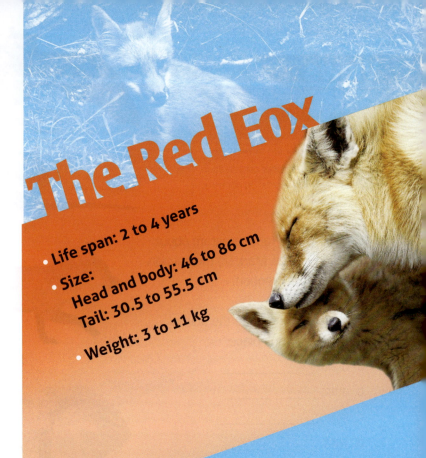

The Red Fox

- Life span: 2 to 4 years
- Size:
  Head and body: 46 to 86 cm
  Tail: 30.5 to 55.5 cm
- Weight: 3 to 11 kg

Red foxes live all around the world in different habitats, including large cities. They make their dens underground and the female typically has two to twelve cubs. They eat almost anything, but they prefer meat.

Red foxes hunt well. They are famous for their speed and agility. They run fast (up to 50 kilometers per hour) to catch mice and rabbits. They also have an excellent sense of smell. When they find a small animal that they can eat, they move quietly to avoid detection. They use their eyes and ears to find the animal's exact location. They watch the animal carefully to see if there is danger. Then they attack suddenly.

Red foxes also eat fruit and vegetables. In cities, they visit people's yards at night to eat pet food or garbage. However, they are shy and hide to avoid contact with humans.

Grammar > Infinitives (Purpose)

1 Read the examples from the red fox profile and underline the correct options.

> They visit people's yards at night <u>to eat pet food</u>.
> They are shy and hide <u>to avoid contact with humans</u>.
> They move quietly <u>to avoid detection</u>.
> They watch the animal carefully <u>to see if there is danger</u>.
> See *Grammar Reference*, page 106.

a. The underlined words describe the *reason/time* the fox does something.
b. In these cases, we use the *gerund/infinitive* form of the verb.

2 Underline two more infinitives of purpose in the red fox profile.

3 Match what the animals do to the reasons.

a. Monkeys climb
b. Kangaroos use a pocket
c. Chameleons change color
d. Bears sleep all winter
e. Dogs bark
f. Zebras run

___ to escape from danger.
___ to find food in trees.
___ to save energy.
___ to blend in with the surroundings.
___ to carry their babies.
___ to get their owner's attention.

Writing > An Animal Profile

> Use the prompts to write a profile about coyotes.

Coyotes

- **Life span: 10 to 14 years**
- **Size: 58 to 66 cm**
- **Weight: 7 to 21 kg**

- Live / different habitats including grasslands, deserts, around urban areas
- Live in packs / 4–7 pups in a litter / dig dens for young
- Eat rodents, fruit, garbage, small animals
- Run up to 70 kilometers per hour to escape danger
- Work in teams to escape danger

Unit 5 57

Out and About

Reading > **In the Wild**

1 Skim the article on page 59 quickly and underline what it is about.

   a. Taking great photos of animals
   b. Shooting animals in the wild
   c. Taking better pictures

2 Label the tips in the article with the headings in the box.

   | Use camouflage   Research   Be patient |

3 Number the information in the order it appears in the article.

   ___ Why it is important to read about animals before you come
   ___ The advantages of wildlife sanctuaries
   ___ The description of the contest prize
   ___ Who Kat Jenkins is
   ___ Why the photographer is using camouflage

Vocabulary > **Prepositions of Place**

1 Look at the picture and complete the description with the prepositions in the box.

   | on   in   under   in front of
   next to   above   across   behind |

There is a snake 1) _____ the car. A lion is 2) _____ the car and a crocodile is 3) _____ it. The elephant is 4) _____ the car and a hippo is 5) _____ the elephant. There is a giraffe 6) _____ the car. A vulture is flying in circles 7) _____ the car. The photographer is 8) _____ the river.

2 Listen and check your answers.

Listening > **Animals in the Wild**

1 Listen to a radio broadcaster on safari. Mark (✓) the animals that he mentions.

   a. Crocodile ___
   b. Zebra ___
   c. Lion ___
   d. Vulture ___

2 Listen again and mark the sentences *T* (true) or *F* (false).

   a. Vultures are in the water. ___
   b. The zebras see the crocodiles. ___
   c. The zebras want to drink water. ___
   d. The zoologist is up in a tree. ___
   e. The zebras run away. ___

How to Take an Amazing Shot

There is still time to send in your wildlife photos for *Nature Journal*'s annual contest. In this issue, last year's winner gives tips for taking wildlife pictures.

Kat Jenkins is a wildlife photographer. She especially loves taking pictures on safaris. Many countries have wildlife sanctuaries that promote safari vacations. These bring in money and help to protect endangered species. But it is not easy to take good pictures of animals, especially wild ones.

At the moment, Kat is shooting a wildlife documentary and writing a book on African wildlife. So what are her top tips for taking great wildlife pictures?

Tip 2: _____

Look carefully at this picture. The monkeys are grooming each other. The photographer is hiding in a tree. She is wearing special clothes to hide herself. She looks like part of the tree.

Tip 1: _____

Read about the animal before you go. That way, you have an idea of how the animal behaves and you have a better chance of getting good pictures. In this picture, the photographer did her research. She is in the right place at the right time. The monarch butterflies are arriving to spend the winter. She is taking the picture from below.

Tip 3: _____

This is an incredible shot. The zebras are drinking water and a lion is attacking one of the zebras. An elephant is standing in front of the zebras. The photographer waited for the zebras for days to get her picture. She was lucky, but she was also very patient.

Follow Kat's tips, send in your photos, and win! This year's prize is a safari to Kruger National Park in South Africa.

Grammar > Present Continuous

1 Read the examples from *Track 29* and mark (✓) how we use the present continuous.

> *A group of zebras is arriving now.*
> *What are they doing?*
> *The zebra isn't looking around.*
>
> See *Grammar Reference*, page 106.

  a. To describe actions in progress at or around the moment of speaking. ___
  b. To describe a completed action. ___

2 Underline the correct options to complete the rules.

  a. We form the present continuous with the auxiliary verb *to be/to do* + *-ing* form of the main verb.
  b. We form the negative by adding *not* (*n't*) *before/after* the auxiliary verb.
  c. The position of the subject *changes/does not change* in questions.

3 Complete the phone conversation with the correct form of the verb *to be*.

MAGGIE: What 1) _____ the animals doing?

JOSH: The elephants 2) _____ taking a bath.

MAGGIE: 3) _____ Craig taking pictures with you?

JOSH: No, he 4) _____.
He 5) _____ waiting in the car. What are you doing?

MAGGIE: I 6) _____ not doing anything special. I 7) _____ watching a movie.

4 Complete the sentences with the correct form of the words in the box.

| take   not watch   clean   hunt   follow |

  a. The guide _____ the tourists to see lions.
  b. The lion cub _____ its mother to the watering hole.
  c. The mother lion _____ her cub. She _____ zebras.
  d. The monkeys in the tree _____ each other.

5 Look at the pictures. Use the prompts to write sentences about what the people and animals are doing.

(run away from/elephant)
(chase/monkey)
(play/tablet)
(shout/woman)
(take photo/hippo)

Speaking > Describing a Picture

> Work in pairs. Find the differences in the pictures.
Student A: Turn to page 93.
Student B: Turn to page 95.

60 Unit 5

Review

1 Complete the sentences that describe the picture with the prepositions in the box.

| on | in | under | beside | above |

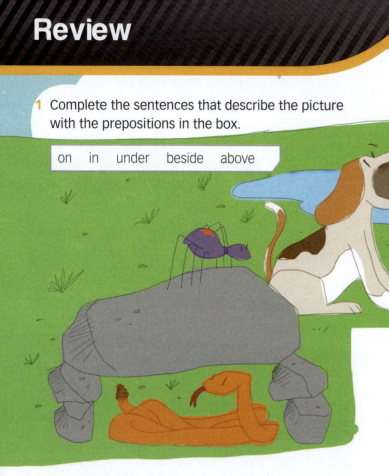

a. The dog is _____ the cat.
b. The snake is _____ the rock.
c. The spider is _____ the rock.
d. The bird is _____ the tree.
e. The fish are _____ the water.

> In your notebook, write what the animals are doing.

2 Complete the pet questionnaire with the correct form of the verbs in parentheses.

What pet is for you?

a. Do you love _____ (take) care of animals?
b. Do you like _____ (have) a pet to keep you company?
c. Do you enjoy _____ (go) for long walks?
d. Do you like _____ (play) with animals?
e. Do you enjoy _____ (have) something to keep you busy?

If your answer is *yes* to all of the above, a dog is for you!

3 Use the prompts to write sentences.

a. communicate / Birds / chirp / to
_____
b. Lionesses / feed / hunt / their cubs / to
_____
c. stay / climb / to / safe / Monkeys / trees
_____
d. attention / meow / get / Cats / to
_____

4 Read the text about dogs and say why they deserve to be treated well.

Our best friends!

Dogs like being with people and many people like having a dog. Dogs are good company. But more than good company, they are also good for our health. Dogs like going for walks with their owners. They love taking long walks in the park. This is a good way for pet owners to keep fit and to meet people. Dogs help people to socialize. Studies also show that they help people to relax. Some dogs help people in other ways too. Guide dogs help blind people to live independently. They are our best friends and deserve to be treated well.

> Write a similar paragraph about another pet. Describe its character and the type of person who likes having it as a pet.

Unit 5

6 The USA

Value Liberty Where liberty is, there is my country

1. Work in pairs. Use the prompts to talk about your town and country.
   - A famous monument in your town or state
   - A famous person in the history of your country
   - An important national holiday

2. Share your answers with the class.

Welcome to Mount Rushmore

Mount Rushmore, in South Dakota, is one of the greatest attractions in the United States. Join over two million annual visitors at the site of this incredible mountain memorial. The monument features the sculptures of the heads of four United States presidents. George Washington, Thomas Jefferson, Abraham Lincoln, and Theodore Roosevelt were all important American presidents. George Washington was the first president. Thomas Jefferson was the third president and also the principal author of the Declaration of Independence, written in 1776. Abraham Lincoln was the sixteenth president. He was famous for ending slavery in 1865. Theodore Roosevelt was the twenty-sixth president. He was president from 1901 to 1909 and was famous for creating the National Park system in the United States.

My World

Reading > Mount Rushmore

Using Your Knowledge of Places
Before reading a text about places, think about what you know about them. This will help give you some context.

1. Look at the brochure and answer the questions.
   a. What famous national monument can you see?
   b. Where is it and what does it represent?

2. Read the brochure and write what the numbers and dates refer to.
   a. 1776: _____
   b. 1865: _____
   c. 21: _____
   d. 18: _____
   e. October 4, 1927: _____
   f. December 25: _____

3. Write where you can do things at the park.
   a. Eat lunch
   _____
   b. Buy a souvenir to take home
   _____
   c. Learn about the history of the monument
   _____
   d. Buy a book about Mount Rushmore
   _____

Vocabulary > Dates

1. Number the months in order.
   ___ October   ___ September
   ___ February   ___ August
   ___ January   ___ July
   ___ June   ___ December
   ___ May   ___ November
   ___ April   ___ March

Interesting Facts

- The presidents' heads are sixty feet tall.
- Washington's nose is twenty-one feet long.
- The other presidents' noses are twenty feet long, their eyes are about eleven feet wide, and their mouths are approximately eighteen feet wide.
- Work on the heads started on October 4, 1927. The project was finally completed in October, 1941.

Park Facilities

After you visit the sculptures, come to our Visitor's Center and learn more about the lives of the presidents and the creators of the monument. In addition to the Lincoln Borglum Museum and Visitor Center, there is also the Buffalo Dining Room and Gift Shop. The museum has exhibits, two theaters, a bookstore, and interactive displays about the construction and history of the monument. Speak to a tour guide for more information.

Opening Hours

The park is open every day of the year, except December 25.

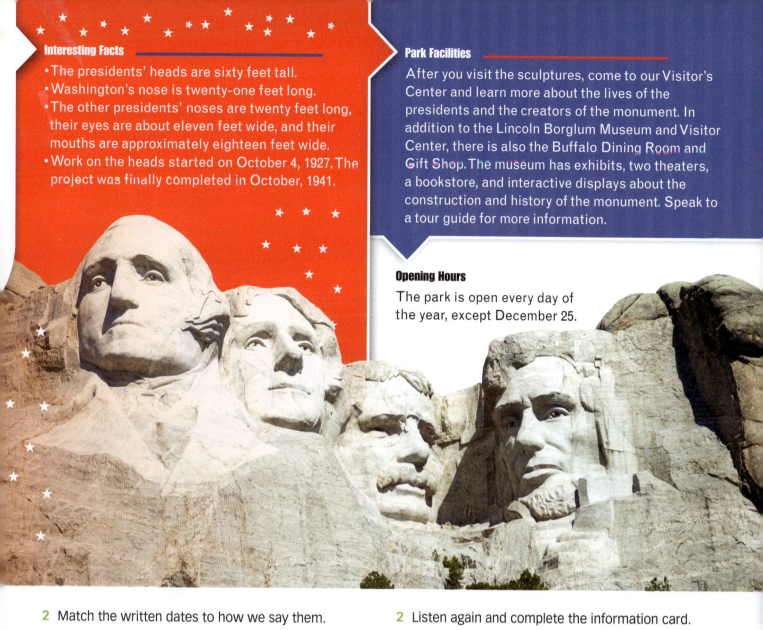

2 Match the written dates to how we say them.

a. May 15th   d. 10/27
b. July 4th   e. 1999
c. March 10, 1990   f. 3/18/2010

___ nineteen ninety-nine
___ October twenty-seventh
___ March eighteenth, two thousand and ten/twenty ten
___ the fourth of July/July fourth
___ May fifteenth
___ March tenth, nineteen ninety

Listening › Building Mount Rushmore

1 Listen to a guide answering tourists' questions. Number the questions in order.

___ Were there any accidents?
___ Who was the sculptor of the heads?
___ Were local people happy with the monument?
___ Was he the only sculptor on the project?
___ Was he American?

2 Listen again and complete the information card.

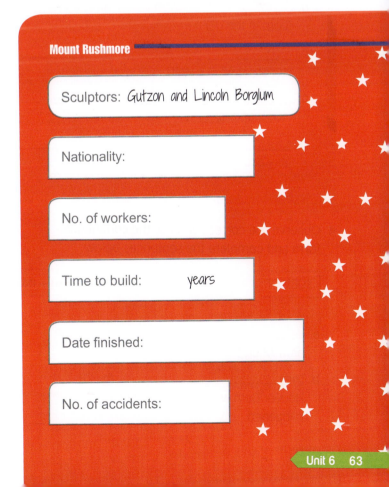

Mount Rushmore

Sculptors: Gutzon and Lincoln Borglum

Nationality:

No. of workers:

Time to build: years

Date finished:

No. of accidents:

Unit 6   63

Grammar > To be (Simple Past and Past Continuous)

1 Read the examples from *Track 30* and underline the verb *to be*.

> Who was the sculptor?
> The sculptor was Gutzon Borglum.
> Was he American?
> Yes, he was. His parents were immigrants from Denmark.
> Was he the only sculptor on the project?
> No, he wasn't.
> Were there any accidents?
> No, there weren't.
>
> See *Grammar Reference*, page 107.

2 Match the phrases to complete the rules.

a. The simple past tense of *to be* is

b. We use *was* with *I*, *he*, *she,* and *it*

c. To form the negative, we put

d. To form a question, we put

___ and *were* with *you*, *we*, and *they*.

___ *was* or *were* before the subject.

___ *was* or *were*.

___ *not* after *was* or *were*.

3 Look at the information card and use the prompts to write questions.

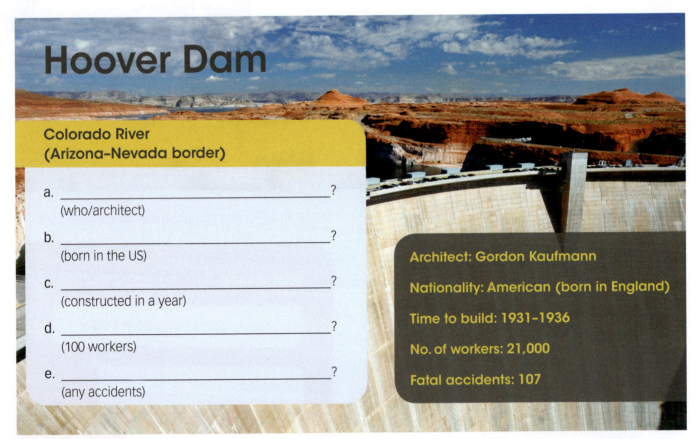

Hoover Dam

Colorado River (Arizona-Nevada border)

a. _____? (who/architect)

b. _____? (born in the US)

c. _____? (constructed in a year)

d. _____? (100 workers)

e. _____? (any accidents)

Architect: Gordon Kaufmann

Nationality: American (born in England)

Time to build: 1931–1936

No. of workers: 21,000

Fatal accidents: 107

4 Observe the correct order of the continuous form and complete the sentences below:

| SUBJECT | + | VERB TO BE (PAST) | + | VERB + ING |

a. He _____ (present) the area when the workers arrived.

b. They _____ (build) Hoover Dam when many accidents happened.

Speaking > Famous People

> Work in pairs. Find out about other monuments to famous people around the world.

Student A: Turn to page 93.
Student B: Turn to page 95.

Views

Listening > The American Dream

Listening for Specific Information
When listening for specific information, listen carefully for that information only. Do not worry if you do not understand everything.

1 Look at the pictures and answer the questions.

a. Who are the people getting off the boat?

b. Where are they going? Why?

c. What do the famous people in the other pictures have in common with the people in the first picture?

2 Listen 🎧 to the first part of a radio program about the "American dream" and check your guesses.

3 Listen 🎧 to the second part of the radio program and underline the correct options to complete the sentences.

a. The speaker's grandmother lived in…
   1. Germany.
   2. England.
   3. Italy.

b. After she arrived in the US, she worked in…
   1. hotels.
   2. stores.
   3. restaurants.

c. A Hollywood agent called her and offered her…
   1. a place to live.
   2. a job as an actress.
   3. a job as a singer.

d. The grandfather escaped from…
   1. the Russians.
   2. the French.
   3. the Nazis.

e. He worked as a…
   1. police officer.
   2. taxi driver.
   3. student.

f. He started work as a doctor…
   1. when he arrived in the US.
   2. after he graduated.
   3. before he graduated.

Pronunciation > /t/, /d/, /id/

1 Listen 🎧 to the pronunciation of the final -ed of the words in the table.

/d/	/t/	/id/
lived	worked	started
phoned	escaped	wanted

2 Add the simple past tense form of the verbs to the table according to how we pronounce the final -ed.

> like   graduate   move   arrive   invite
> continue   wait   look   watch

3 Listen 🎧 and check. Then work in pairs to practice saying the words aloud.

Unit 6 65

Vocabulary > **Jobs**

1. Listen to the people describing their jobs and number them in order.

   a. ___ actor: _____
   b. ___ taxi driver: _____
   c. ___ politician: _____
   d. ___ server: _____
   e. ___ doctor: _____
   f. ___ musician: _____
   g. ___ teacher: _____
   h. ___ artist: _____

2. Listen again and write the speakers' nationalities. Then work in pairs to identify them.

   The teacher was French.
   No, he/she wasn't. The teacher was German.

Reading > **A Famous Immigrant**

1. Discuss the questions with your colleagues.

   a. Who was Albert Einstein?
   b. Where was he from?
   c. Which of these was he: a biologist, a chemist, or a physicist?
   d. Where did he die?

2. Read the biography and check your answers.

3. Write the events of Albert Einstein's life on the time line.

BIOGRAPHY
Albert Einstein

Albert Einstein was a very important scientist. He developed the theory of relativity. He was born on March 14, 1879, in Germany. He studied at a secondary school in Munich. He enjoyed his classes and was a good student, but he disliked the strict discipline. He stopped going to that school when he was fifteen.

Albert Einstein's family moved to Pavia, Italy, in 1894. He finished high school in Switzerland and entered a science school. When he finished, a friend helped him to find a job as a clerk in the Swiss Federal Patent Office in Bern. Einstein worked at the patent office from 1902 to 1909. Those years were very productive for Einstein. The job allowed him time for physics and he published his greatest works.

Einstein visited the United States for the first time in 1921. He was in the US again in 1933, when Adolf Hitler came to power in Germany. Einstein decided not to return to Europe. He eventually decided to become a United States citizen in October of 1940. He died in Princeton, New Jersey, on April 18, 1955.

Born in Germany

March 1879

_____

1894

_____

1902

_____

1921

_____

1940

_____

1955

Grammar > Simple Past (Regular Verbs)

1 Read the excerpt from the text about Einstein and underline the verbs in the past.

> Albert Einstein studied at a secondary school in Munich. He enjoyed his classes and was a good student, but he disliked the strict discipline. He stopped going to that school when he was fifteen. He moved to Pavia, Italy, in 1894.
>
> See *Grammar Reference*, page 107.

2 Match the sentence halves to complete the rules.

a. The simple past describes…
b. We add -ed…
c. If the verb ends in *e*,…
d. If the verb ends in a vowel and a consonant,…
e. If the verb ends in a consonant + *y*,…

___ we add -d.
___ we eliminate the *y* and add -ied.
___ finished past actions.
___ to regular verbs.
___ we double the consonant and add -ed.

3 Write the past tense form of the verbs.

a. marry–_____
b. study–_____
c. stop–_____
d. chat–_____
e. listen–_____
f. want–_____
g. escape–_____
h. decide–_____

4 Complete Alexander Graham Bell's biography with the correct form of the verbs in the box.

| study | move | open | emigrate | invent |

Alexander Graham Bell

Alexander Graham Bell was born on March 3, 1847, in Edinburgh, Scotland. He 1) _____ anatomy and physiology there and in London. In 1870, Bell 2) _____ with his family to Canada. Then, the following year, he 3) _____ to the United States to teach. In 1872, Bell 4) _____ a school in Boston to train teachers of the deaf. He is most famous for his work on the telephone, which he 5) _____ in 1876. He became a US citizen in 1882.

Writing > A Biography

> Write a short biography about a famous person or someone you know whose life you find interesting or extraordinary.

Writing a Biography
- Use the simple past to describe finished actions or events.
- List events chronologically.

Unit 6

Out and About

AMERICAN HISTORY: The Boston Tea Party

In December 1773, three British ships arrived in Boston, Massachusetts, with loads of tea. The American colonists protested. They did not want to pay a British tax on tea. For the colonists, this was another example of "taxation without representation" from a government thousands of miles away. However, the British governor, Thomas Hutchinson, tried to force them to pay.

On the night of December 16, a group of colonists painted their faces and dressed in the clothes of Mohawk Indians. Then they boarded the British ships, captured the sailors, and dumped all the tea into the harbor.

The British government in London was very angry. It closed Boston Harbor and created a new administration in Massachusetts with only British officials. It also forced American families to accept British soldiers into their houses and give them food and places to sleep.

The colonists were angry and called the treatment intolerable. They organized the First Continental Congress in 1774, and representatives from twelve colonies attended. They decided to stop buying British products and they promised to defend Massachusetts if the British attacked. They also started to collect weapons to fight the British. When the British tried to destroy the colonists' weapons, the colonists resisted and many soldiers died. That was the start of the American War of Independence.

Put this on.

Paint your face.

Reading > The Boston Tea Party

1 Look at the text and the pictures and underline what the Boston Tea Party was.
   a. A sports competition
   b. A celebration
   c. A rebellion

2 Read the article and mark the sentences T (true) or F (false).
   a. The colonists didn't like tea. ___
   b. They asked the governor to throw the tea into the harbor. ___
   c. The British were happy with the colonists. ___
   d. The First Continental Congress was in 1775. ___
   e. Only Massachusetts' colonists attended the Congress. ___
   f. The colonists started to prepare for war. ___

3 Match the words from the article to the definitions.
   a. Tax   ___ n. a person who works on a ship
   b. To board   ___ v. to throw something away
   c. To dump   ___ n. money people pay to the government
   d. Sailor   ___ n. a place for ships to stay safely
   e. Harbor   ___ v. to go onto a ship or airplane
   f. Weapon   ___ n. a thing people use to fight

Vocabulary > Cognates

1 Underline the words that have a similar form and meaning in your language (cognates).

doctor   nurse   hospital   tourist
university   family   brother   active
delicious   impossible   beautiful   stupid
negotiate   insist   speak   imagine

2 Underline more cognates in the article.

3 Complete the sentences with the correct form of cognates from the article and from activity 1.
   a. People often _____ in the streets when they are not happy about something.
   b. Tax conditions for the colonists were _____.
   c. Thomas Hutchinson _____ that the colonists pay.
   d. The British did not want to _____ with the colonists.
   e. Today, the Boston Tea Party Ships and Museum is popular with _____.

68   Unit 6

Listening 〉 The War of Independence

1. Work in pairs. Look at the picture and discuss what it represents.

2. Listen to a game show and underline the correct answers.

a. When did the American War of Independence start?
   1. In 1761.
   2. In 1775.
   3. In 1789.

b. When did the colonists declare independence?
   1. On July 4, 1776.
   2. On July 4, 1789.
   3. On July 4, 1804.

3. Listen again and answer the questions.

a. Where did the war start?
   _____

b. How long did the war last?
   _____

c. What peace treaty did the Americans and British sign?
   _____

Unit 6   69

Grammar — Simple Past (Negative, Questions, and Short Answers)

1 Look at the examples from *Track 36*. Underline the auxiliary verbs and circle the main verbs.

> When did the war start?
> Did it start in 1775? Yes, it did.
> Where did it start? It started in Boston.
> No, it didn't! It didn't start in Boston.
> See *Grammar Reference*, page 108.

2 Read the examples in activity 1 again and underline the correct options to complete the rules.

a. We use the auxiliary verb *did/was* in negatives and questions in the simple past.

b. We use the *simple past/base form* of the main verb in negatives and questions in the simple past.

c. For questions, we *change/do not change* the position of the subject and auxiliary verb.

d. We use the *auxiliary/main* verb in short answers.

3 Study the time line about the American Civil War and write short answers to the questions.

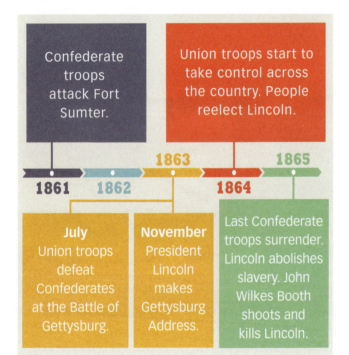

a. Did the war start in 1862?
_____

b. Did Lincoln make the Gettysburg Address?
_____

c. Did Union troops shoot Lincoln?
_____

d. Did Confederate troops surrender?
_____

e. Did John Wilkes Booth abolish slavery?
_____

Speaking — History Quiz

1 Work in groups. Choose a historical event from your country and make notes about it.

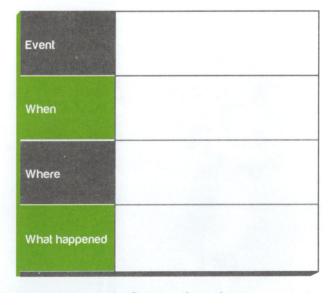

4 Use the prompts to write more questions about the time line.

a. when / Lincoln / Gettysburg Address / make
_____?

b. where / Civil War / start
_____?

c. did / Lincoln / win election / 1863
_____?

d. what / Lincoln / abolish
_____?

e. when / Civil War / end
_____?

2 In your group, write five questions about your event.

3 Use the questions to quiz another group.

Review

1. Listen to a teen describing important dates in her life. Complete the information.

   a. My birthday is on _____.

   b. My sister's birthday is in _____.

   c. My dad's birthday is on _____.

   d. My mom's birthday is in _____.

2. Complete the text with the correct form of the verbs in parentheses.

   My grandmother's name 1) _____ (be) Sally and my grandfather's name 2) _____ (be) Sam. They 3) _____ (be not) American. She 4) _____ (be) Chilean and he 5) _____ (be) Brazilian. When she 6) _____ (arrive) in the US, my grandmother 7) _____ (call) her sister. Her sister wasn't at home, so my grandmother 8) _____ (decide) to take a taxi. The taxi 9) _____ (stop) at the house, but it 10) _____ (be) the wrong address. My grandmother 11) _____ (start) to cry. The taxi driver 12) _____ (like) my grandmother. He 13) _____ (invite) her to have a coffee. My grandmother 14) _____ (marry) the taxi driver two years after that.

   > Work in pairs. Write a biography of a person in your family. Describe the people you wrote about.

3. Complete the interview with the correct form of the verbs in parentheses.

   A: When 1) _____ you _____ (arrive) in the US?

   B: I 2) _____ (arrive) in 1963.

   A: 3) _____ you _____ (live) in New York at the time?

   B: Yes, I 4) _____ (do).

   A: When 5) _____ you _____ (move) to Hollywood?

   B: I 6) _____ (move) in 1964.

   A: 7) _____ you _____ (work) as an actress from the very beginning?

   B: No, I 8) _____ (do). I 9) _____ (be) a server for a while.

4. Read the text and answer the questions.

   a. Who is the person on the coin?

   b. Why is he famous?

   c. How did he die?

   ### John Fitzgerald Kennedy

   There are many memorials to John F. Kennedy in the United States. For example, New York's international airport is called JFK, and the name of NASA's main operations center is the John F. Kennedy Space Center.

   John F. Kennedy was the president of the United States from 1961 to 1963. He and his wife, Jackie, were very popular. John descended from a family of immigrants who arrived in the US around 1850. They were poor farmers from Ireland, but they worked very hard to be successful.

   John F. Kennedy died in 1963 in Dallas, Texas. He was the victim of an assassination.

> Write about a memorial to a famous person in your country's history.

Unit 6   71

7 Story Time

Value Creativity Connecting things in a new way

1 Match the columns. Say how they are related.

a. ghost ☐ hare (rabbit)
b. full moon ☐ wolf
c. tortoise ☐ castle

2 Work in groups. Find someone who made different connections.

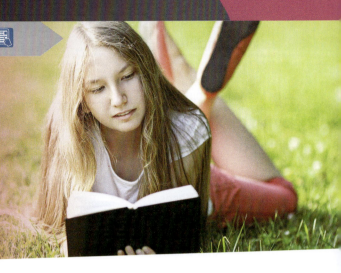

My World

Reading ▶ Fahrenheit 451

Pronoun Reference
Writers often use pronouns to avoid repeating names and words. It is important to know who or what the pronouns refer to when you read.

1 Work in pairs. Mark (✓) the types of books you like to read and discuss your favorite types of stories.

a. science fiction ___
b. horror ___
c. adventure ___
d. romance ___
e. comedy ___
f. mystery ___

2 Skim the book summary quickly and label it with the correct type of book from activity 1.

☐ Fahrenheit 451

Fahrenheit 451 is a novel by Ray Bradbury. It presents a vision of a future American society.

The book is about Guy Montag, a firefighter who doesn't put out fires—<u>he</u> starts them. Guy burns books. He lives in a city of the future where the
5   government prohibits books because it thinks <u>they</u> are dangerous. The title of the novel is *Fahrenheit 451* because this is the temperature at which paper burns.

At first, Guy enjoys his job, but one day, on his way home from work, he meets his neighbor Clarisse, who tells him that <u>she</u> loves reading. She
10   tells him about her favorite books. After that, Guy goes home, where he tries to chat with his wife, but she does not want to talk to him. <u>She</u> spends the day watching TV. Guy decides not to burn a book, but to read it instead. He realizes books are not dangerous and that his society is not perfect.

15   Then, one day at work, an old woman refuses to leave her books and she dies in the fire. Guy saves some books from the woman's house and takes them home. His wife suspects that he is secretly reading, so she tells the government. Other firefighters visit his home. They find the books and burn <u>them</u>, but Guy escapes.

20   Next, Guy discovers a community outside of the city where everyone reads books. A war starts in the city and destroys it. In the end, Guy returns to the city with his new friends to build a better society.

3 Underline the words the pronouns refer to.

a. "He" in line 3 refers to…
1. the book.
2. Montag.
3. Bradbury.

b. "They" in line 5 refers to…
1. firefighters.
2. governments.
3. books.

c. "She" in line 9 refers to…
1. Clarisse.
2. an old woman.
3. Guy's wife.

d. "She" in line 12 refers to…
1. Clarisse.
2. an old woman.
3. Guy's wife.

e. "Them" in line 19 refers to…
1. firefighters.
2. the government.
3. the books.

4 Answer the questions.

a. Why is Guy different from most firefighters?
_____

b. How is Clarisse different from Guy's wife?
_____

c. What does Guy learn from reading the book?
_____

d. Why does the old woman die in the fire?
_____

e. What is special about the community Guy goes to?
_____

Vocabulary > Sequencing Words

1 Find and underline the words and phrases in the text.

| at first | then | next | after that | in the end |

2 Number the events in a logical order.

____ Guy returns to the city with some new friends.
____ He meets Clarisse. She tells him about books.
____ Guy is not a normal firefighter. He burns books.
____ Guy reads some books and decides to leave his job.
____ His wife tells the government and Guy leaves the city.

Listening > Talking about Books

1 Work in groups. Find out what your classmates know about the books in the pictures.

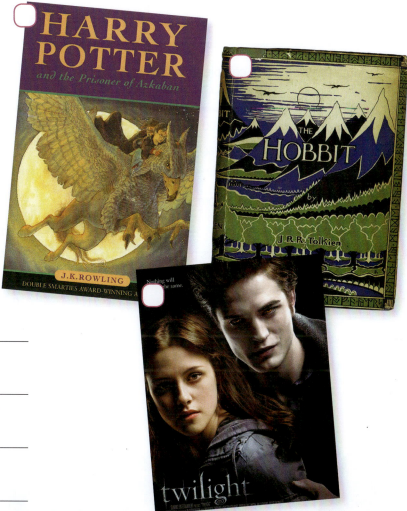

2 Listen 🎧 to two teens discussing a book. Mark (✓) the one they talk about.

3 Listen again and mark the sentences T (true) or F (false).

a. The book is about two teens who fall in love. ____
b. Edward stops a bus that almost hits Bella. ____
c. James is a vampire that wants to hurt Bella. ____
d. Bella goes to a hotel, where she hides. ____

Unit 7 73

Grammar > Relative Clauses (Who/That/Where)

1 Read the examples from *Track 38* and complete the table with the underlined relative pronouns.

> *Bella is a shy girl* <u>who</u> *moves to a new school,* <u>where</u> *she meets a boy.*
> *He's a vampire. A special kind of vampire* <u>that</u> *only drinks animal blood.*
> *He stops a car* <u>that</u> *almost hits her.*
>
> See *Grammar Reference*, page 108.

People	Things	People and things	Places
who			

2 Match the clauses to complete the sentences.

a. Harry Potter is a boy
b. Hogwarts is a special school
c. Snape is the name of a teacher
d. Hermione is a girl
e. Platform 9 3/4 is the platform
f. Quidditch is a game

___ that students at Hogwarts play.
___ where the Hogwarts Express departs from.
___ who learns he is a wizard.
___ who Harry meets on the train.
___ who teaches at Hogwarts.
___ where they teach magic.

3 Use *who*, *that*, or *where* to complete the sentences.

a. Ron Weasley is a boy _____ helps Harry.
b. The students go to a classroom _____ they learn about magic potions.
c. Snape is a teacher _____ doesn't like Harry.
d. Harry has a magic cloak _____ makes him invisible.
e. Voldemort is an evil wizard _____ killed Harry's parents.
f. Harry fights with Voldemort in a room _____ there is a magic stone.

4 Write sentences containing relative clauses. Use *who*, *that*, or *where*.

a. Harry and Ron go back to school in a car. The car flies.
   _____
b. Draco Malfoy is a boy. He is Harry's enemy.
   _____
c. Harry finds a diary. The diary belongs to a ghost.
   _____
d. Harry and Ron go into a forest. Giant spiders attack them there.
   _____
e. Hagrid is a giant. He helps Harry and Ron.
   _____
f. Harry enters the Chamber of Secrets. He fights with a giant snake there.
   _____

Views

Listening > A Voice in the Night

Listening for Important Information in a Story
When listening to a story, ask yourself: Who are the main characters? Where does the story take place? What are the main events? This will help you to understand the context.

1. Work in pairs. Look at the picture and answer the questions.
   a. Where does the story take place?
   b. Who do you think the main characters are?

2. Listen to the story and underline the sentence that summarizes it best.
   a. It is about a boy who finds a strange watch.
   b. It is about a boy who encounters a ghost while on vacation.
   c. It is about a boy who gets lost in a forest.

3. Listen again and number the main events in order.
   ___ He found a watch in his room.
   ___ He arrived at the cabin.
   ___ He saw water on the floor.
   ___ He took off his watch and went swimming.
   ___ He heard a loud noise and woke up.

4. Answer the questions.
   a. What did the boy hear when they arrived?
   _____
   b. Why did he take off his watch?
   _____
   c. What did his dad say after the boy woke up?
   _____
   d. What did the owner of the cabin tell the boy and his father?
   _____

Pronunciation > Rhythm

1. Listen and notice how the speaker stresses the underlined words.
   a. We <u>stayed</u> in a <u>cabin</u> at a <u>campsite</u>.
   b. It was a <u>beautiful place</u>.
   c. I <u>wanted</u> to <u>swim</u>.
   d. I <u>went</u> to my <u>room</u>.
   e. My <u>watch</u> was on the <u>table</u>.

2. Listen again and repeat the sentences aloud.

3. Underline the words that carry the stress in these sentences. Then listen and check.
   a. We traveled by train to the beach.
   b. It was an expensive restaurant.
   c. He loved to paint.
   d. I ate on the patio.
   e. Her shoes are next to the bed.

Vocabulary > Adjective Opposites

1. Match the adjectives to their opposites.
   a. good   ___ large
   b. small   ___ hot
   c. quiet   ___ bad
   d. cold   ___ happy
   e. sad   ___ loud

2. Work in pairs. Write the adjectives next to the things they describe in the story.
   a. _____ cabin
   b. _____ lake
   c. _____ cocoa
   d. _____ time
   e. _____ water
   f. _____ noise
   g. _____ room
   h. _____ dream
   i. _____ story
   j. _____ boy

Speaking > Favorite Books

1. Work in pairs. Come to a consensus about three books you would take with you to a desert island. Give reasons for your choices.

2. Work with another pair. Decide on a group list of three books.

Unit 7 75

Reading > A Haunted Castle

1. Read the story and number the pictures in order.

2. Match the pictures to the captions.
   a. He saw a white figure. ___
   b. They met the owner. ___
   c. He took off the sheet. ___
   d. He ran out of the room. ___
   e. The owner told ghost stories. ___

3. Write notes in the story map.

Setting (when, where)
Halloween, an old castle.
Characters (who)
Plot (what happened)
Conclusion (ending)

FRIGHT NIGHT

One Halloween, some friends named Simon and Emily went to stay in an old castle. The owner met them and took them to their rooms. They put their bags in their rooms and then went down to eat. They ate at a large wooden table with candles. The owner told ghost stories. After dinner, Simon told Emily he did not believe in ghosts. Later, they said good night and went to their rooms.

Simon didn't sleep well. During the night, he heard a strange noise and woke up. He turned on the light and saw a white figure next to the window. He screamed, got out of bed, and ran out of the room. Emily was in the hallway. "What did you see?" she asked.

"A ghost!" Simon answered. "I saw a ghost!"

"You didn't see a ghost!" a voice said. The castle owner came out of this room carrying a white sheet. "Happy Halloween!" he said. They all laughed.

"I love practical jokes!" said Emily.

"Sure. Easy for you to say!" Simon replied. "I'm still shaking!"

76 Unit 7

Grammar > Simple Past (Irregular Verbs)

1 Read the extract from the ghost story and underline the verbs.

> He turned on the light and saw a white figure next to the window. He screamed, got out of bed, and ran out of the room. Emily was in the hallway. "What did you see?" she asked. "A ghost!" Simon answered. "I saw a ghost!"
> "You didn't see a ghost!" a voice said.

See *Grammar Reference*, page 108.

2 Work in pairs. Discuss the questions.
   a. Which verbs in the extract are regular and which are irregular?
   b. How do we form simple past questions? Is it the same for regular and irregular verbs?
   c. How do we form negative sentences in the simple past? Is the rule the same for regular and irregular verbs?

3 Write the simple past forms of the verbs.
   a. go _____
   b. eat _____
   c. tell _____
   d. sleep _____
   e. hear _____
   f. wake up _____
   g. see _____
   h. have _____
   i. get up _____
   j. run _____
   k. come back _____

4 Complete the story with the correct simple past tense form of the verbs in parentheses.

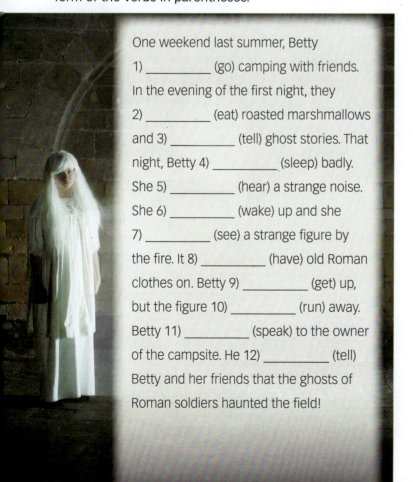

One weekend last summer, Betty 1) _____ (go) camping with friends. In the evening of the first night, they 2) _____ (eat) roasted marshmallows and 3) _____ (tell) ghost stories. That night, Betty 4) _____ (sleep) badly. She 5) _____ (hear) a strange noise. She 6) _____ (wake) up and she 7) _____ (see) a strange figure by the fire. It 8) _____ (have) old Roman clothes on. Betty 9) _____ (get) up, but the figure 10) _____ (run) away. Betty 11) _____ (speak) to the owner of the campsite. He 12) _____ (tell) Betty and her friends that the ghosts of Roman soldiers haunted the field!

Writing > A Ghost Story

> Look at the items and write a ghost story.

Writing a Story
- Give your story a clear structure:
  - A setting (when, where)
  - Characters (who)
  - Main events (what happened)
  - An ending
- Use past tense verbs.

Unit 7 77

Out and About

Reading > **Storytellers**

1. Read the article and underline the best title.
   a. My Favorite Stories
   b. Voices from the Past
   c. The History of the American West

2. Read the article again and write notes in the graphic organizer.

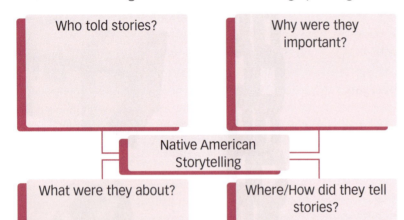

- Who told stories?
- Why were they important?
- What were they about?
- Where/How did they tell stories?

Native American Storytelling

3. Mark the sentences *T* (true) or *F* (false).
   a. Storytellers wrote down the stories. ___
   b. Some stories were educational. ___
   c. The characters were always people. ___
   d. Younger children did not participate in the stories. ___
   e. Storytelling helped preserve a tribe's culture. ___

Vocabulary > **Conjunctions**

1. Underline the conjunctions *and*, *but*, *so*, and *or* in the text.

2. Write the conjunctions beside their functions.
   a. To add something: _____
   b. To give an alternative: _____
   c. To indicate a consequence: _____
   d. To indicate a contrast: _____

Storytelling was a very important tradition in Native American culture in North America. Most tribes did not have a written language, so they used stories to teach children about the history of the tribe and its origins.

Some stories were about brave warriors from the tribe, and people felt proud of their tribe when they heard them. Other stories taught children how to interpret the weather and how to survive in nature. Other stories were funny and used animals as the main characters.

Storytellers were usually older people in the tribe. They often used songs and dances because this made the story more dramatic. They usually told the stories outside, around a fire. Adults and older children participated in the stories, but younger children played or slept in their parents' arms.

Storytelling entertained people and made them feel part of the tribe. Stories passed the history and culture of the tribe to younger people and helped preserve the tribe's values and beliefs. The stories were the voices of past generations.

78 Unit 7

Writing > Story Circle

> Complete the sentences to describe a Native American story circle scene as you imagine it.

a. The storyteller arrived and…
b. A lot of people wanted to listen, so…
c. The older people sat near the fire, but…
d. After the story, people talked or…

Listening > A Traditional Story

1 Listen to a traditional Native American story. Say whether or not your story is similar.

2 Listen again and underline the correct answers to the questions.

a. Who gave the donkey as a gift?
   1. The chief.
   2. The chief's wife.
   3. The boy's grandmother.
b. How old was the boy when he went on the trip?
   1. Two.
   2. Three.
   3. Four.
c. What did the chief want the donkey to carry?
   1. The boy.
   2. The tent.
   3. The boy's grandmother.
d. Why was the donkey angry?
   1. It wanted to carry the boy.
   2. Because of the battle.
   3. Because the tent was heavy.
e. Where were the boy and the donkey after the battle?
   1. At home.
   2. On the battlefield.
   3. With the pony.

3 Mark (✓) the words that best describe the donkey in the story. Give reasons.

a. Proud ___
b. Honorable ___
c. Protective ___
d. Loyal ___

Unit 7 79

Grammar > Past Time Clauses with When

1. Read the examples from *Track 42* and match the clauses to complete the sentences.

   > *The people of the tribe danced and sang* ___
   > *When the boy was two years old,* ___
   > *The donkey got angry* ___
   >
   > See *Grammar Reference,* page 108.

   a. his parents decided to go on a trip.
   b. when they heard the news.
   c. when the chief's wife put the tent on it.

2. Complete the rules.

   a. When the main clause comes first, we *use/don't use* a comma.
   b. When the time clause (with *when*) comes first, we *use/don't use* a comma.

3. Underline the action that happened first in each sentence in activity 1.

4. Look at the pictures and prompts and write sentences using time clauses to complete the traditional story.

   One day, the chief's son and his donkey went fishing…

Review

1 Use the connectors to complete the first part of the book summary.

> because   and   then   but   so   at first

Liesel Meminger was a young German girl who went to live with Hans and Rosa Hubermann in the small town of Molching just before World War II. She went there 1) _____ the Nazis killed her parents. On their way to Molching, Liesel's younger brother Werner died, 2) _____ she felt very sad. 3) _____, Liesel wasn't happy in Molching, 4) _____ Hans Hubermann was very nice to her. He taught her to read. Liesel made friends with a neighborhood boy, Rudy Steiner, who fell in love with her. 5) _____ the wife of the mayor of Molching, Ilsa Hermann, saw Liesel stealing a book. Ilsa liked Liesel, 6) _____ she invited her to read in her library.

2 Complete the sentences about the book with *who*, *where*, and *that*.

  a. Liesel found a book in the cemetery _____ she left her brother.
  b. Hans was a painter _____ also played the accordion.
  c. Hans taught Liesel to read with the book _____ she had found in the cemetery.
  d. Rudy was a boy _____ loved playing games.
  e. Ilsa lived in a house _____ had a large library.

3 Complete the rest of the summary with the correct form of the verbs in parentheses.

The Nazis 1) _____ (be) very cruel to the Jews, so when a Jewish boy named Max 2) _____ (come) to the house, Hans agreed to hide him in the basement. Liesel and Max became good friends. One day, Hans 3) _____ (give) bread to an old Jew who was going to a concentration camp. Max 4) _____ (go) away, and the Nazis forced Hans to join the army, where they gave him a very dangerous job. The Nazis 5) _____ (capture) Max and sent him to a concentration camp. When Liesel 6) _____ (see) him, she felt very upset. She 7) _____ (lose) hope, but Ilsa told her to write her story.
Liesel 8) _____ (write) the story of her life in the Hubermanns' basement, where she survived an attack from the air that 9) _____ (kill) Hans, Rosa, and Rudy. Both Liesel and Max survived the war. In the end, Liesel 10) _____ (have) a long life and died at an old age.

> In your notebook, write a different ending to the story.

4 Read the article. Say why the writer thinks it is good to read fiction.

Why read fiction?

Some people only read factual books. They say they don't learn anything from fiction. But fiction can teach us a lot. It helps us to understand other people better. From the different characters in a book, we learn how other people think. We also experience life in different places and situations, even in different historical times. And very importantly, reading a good story is enjoyable. We want to know what happens next. Finally, when we finish a book, we can talk about it with friends. Fiction is useful and fun!

> Write about another story that teaches about life in an imaginative way.

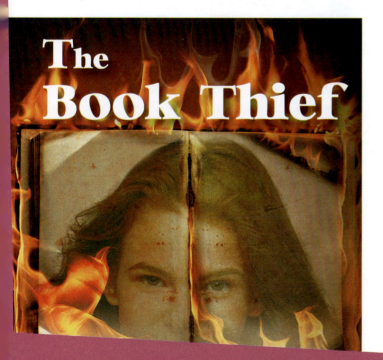

8 Feeling Good

Value Well-being Your health is in your own hands

1. Work in groups. Discuss the questions.
   a. Do you eat healthy food?
   b. Do you get at least eight hours of sleep a night?
   c. Do you exercise regularly?
2. Work in pairs. Discuss why it is important to do the things in activity 1.

My World

Reading > Healthy and Happy

Using a Dictionary
When reading, use an English-Portuguese dictionary to look up unfamiliar words. Some words have several translations. Try out the translations in different sentences to find the one you need.

1. Make a list of your favorite foods.
2. Read the article and check if it mentions the foods you like.

3. Match the foods to their primary effects.
   a. Strawberries and oranges   ___ give us energy
   b. Bananas   ___ help our skin and bones
   c. Pasta and cheese   ___ fight depression
   d. Chocolate   ___ makes us happy

4. Look up the underlined words in the article in a bilingual dictionary and identify the correct translations. Compare your answers in pairs.

Happy eating!
By Hillary Pots

Food is basic to our lives. Without it, our bodies cannot <u>function</u>. Humans <u>cultivate</u> about two thousand different types of plants for food. These include fruit like apples, grapes, and watermelons, as well as vegetables like carrots, onions, and peas. We also consume huge quantities of meat. The average North American eats more than two hundred pounds of meat per year.

However, food has psychological effects too. Fruit like strawberries and oranges contain a lot of vitamin C. This is important for our skin and bones, and also produces endorphins in our brain, which make us feel happy. In addition, endorphins reduce pain and stress and are also an antidepressant. Bananas are rich in potassium, as well as in natural sugars, which make us feel energetic.

The well-known cartoon <u>character</u> Popeye made spinach famous because it gave him incredible strength. However, this leafy vegetable is also full of vitamin B, which helps fight depression. One of the most popular side dishes, pasta and cheese, has the same effect.

A food like chocolate is a special case. Eating a lot of milk chocolate can be bad for our bodies, as it is high in calories, saturated fat, and sugar. But chocolate also makes us feel happy. That is because chocolate increases the levels of endorphins in the brain. Though to get the full <u>effect</u>, the chocolate needs to be at least 70 percent pure cocoa.

So the next time you sit down to eat, remember: what you eat does not just affect your body physically. Food affects your brain too!

5 Answer the questions.
   a. How much meat does an average North American in the US eat every year?
   _____
   b. What do endorphins do?
   _____
   c. What do bananas contain?
   _____
   d. What vegetable helps to fight depression?
   _____
   e. In what ways can chocolate be bad for you?
   _____

Vocabulary > Food

1 Find and underline the foods in the article. Then match them to the pictures.

   a. _____   h. _____
   b. _____   i. _____
   c. _____   j. _____
   d. _____   k. _____
   e. _____   l. _____
   f. _____   m. _____
   g. _____

2 Match the food from activity 1 to the appropriate dishes. Some foods can go in more than one dish.

Fruit Salad
_____
_____

Vegetable Soup
_____
_____

Pizza
_____
_____

Smoothie
_____
_____

Writing > Food Preferences

> Work in pairs. Interview your partner. Then write a short paragraph about his or her food preferences.
   a. How often do you eat fruit?
   b. What's your favorite fruit?
   c. Which vegetables do you like and dislike?
   d. What's your favorite meal time—breakfast, lunch, or dinner?
   e. What is your favorite meal?

Listening > Going Shopping

1 Conduct a survey to find out who does the grocery shopping in your classmates' houses.

2 Listen to two teens doing the grocery shopping and say who sent them shopping.

3 Listen again and complete the shopping list.

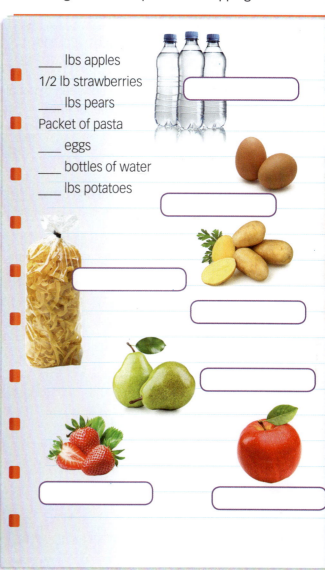

___ lbs apples
1/2 lb strawberries
___ lbs pears
Packet of pasta
___ eggs
___ bottles of water
___ lbs potatoes

4 Label the pictures.

Grammar > Countable and Uncountable Nouns (Some/Any)

1 Work in pairs. Look at the examples from *Track 43* and answer the questions.

> *There's some pasta.*
> *There are some eggs.*
> *Is there any lemonade on the list?*
> *There aren't any chips on Mom's list.*
>
> See *Grammar Reference*, page 108.

a. Can we count pasta?
b. Can we count eggs?
c. Which food items can we count and which can we not count in the article on page 82?

2 Read the examples again and underline the correct options to complete the rules.

a. We use *some/any* in affirmative sentences.
b. We use *some/any* in negative sentences and questions.
c. We use *some/any/both* with plural and noncount nouns.

3 Complete the conversation between two siblings with *is*, *isn't*, *are*, *aren't*, *some*, or *any*.

BROOKE: Joel, 1) _____ there 2) _____ tomatoes in the refrigerator?
JOEL: No, there 3) _____. We don't have 4) _____ tomatoes.
BROOKE: OK, what about peas? Do we have 5) _____ peas?
JOEL: Yes, we have 6) _____ peas.
BROOKE: Good. 7) _____ there 8) _____ cheese?
JOEL: No, there 9) _____. There 10) _____ 11) _____ cheese.
BROOKE: And what about water? 12) _____ there 13) _____ water?
JOEL: No, there 14) _____ 15) _____ water.

4 Look at the pictures and write sentences comparing the list with the food Joel bought.

- Rice
- Sugar
- Pasta
- Tomatoes
- Carrots
- Spinach
- Bread
- Lemons
- Cheese
- Water
- Milk

a. pasta / bread
   He bought some pasta, but he didn't buy any bread.

b. rice / cheese
   _____
   _____

c. carrots / tomatoes
   _____
   _____

d. lemons / strawberries
   _____
   _____

e. milk / ice cream
   _____
   _____

f. spinach / chocolate
   _____
   _____

g. soda / water
   _____
   _____

Unit 8

Views

Listening > Yoga for Teens

Listening to Instructions
When listening to instructions, notice that speakers usually speak more slowly and stress important words. Pay attention to the stressed words to understand the instructions.

1 Read the flier for yoga classes and underline the benefits it mentions.

2 Listen to 🎧44 the instructor's first class and number the poses in the order the students do them.

Yoga for Teens!

After-School Yoga Classes

Thursday 5–6 p.m. with Michael O'Connor

Feeling stressed? No time to sit quietly and think? Yoga helps you to relax and feel better. It improves your balance and concentration. It tones your body and strengthens leg and stomach muscles. Our classes are simple and fun. So come along and try!

3 Listen again and match the instructions to the people they are directed to.

a. John ____ close your eyes
b. Mary ____ breathe quietly
c. Joe ____ move slowly
d. Sonia ____ concentrate

Pronunciation > /æ/ and /ʌ/

1 Listen 🎧45 and notice the sound of the vowels.

/æ/ hat, class, bag
/ʌ/ cup, fun, but

2 Say the words aloud and write them in the correct tables.

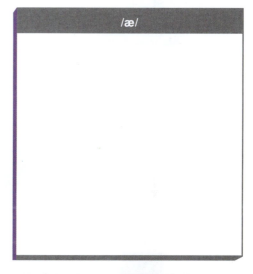

hand last up jump dancer
cat us young back duck
travel cut man summer luck

/æ/

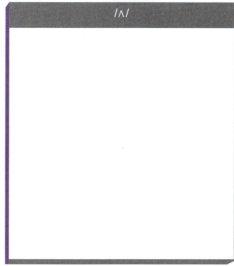

/ʌ/

3 Listen 🎧46 to the words and check your answers.

Unit 8   85

Vocabulary > Parts of the Body

> Label the parts of the body with the words in the box.

head	arm	hand	leg	foot
neck	knee	ankle	shoulder	

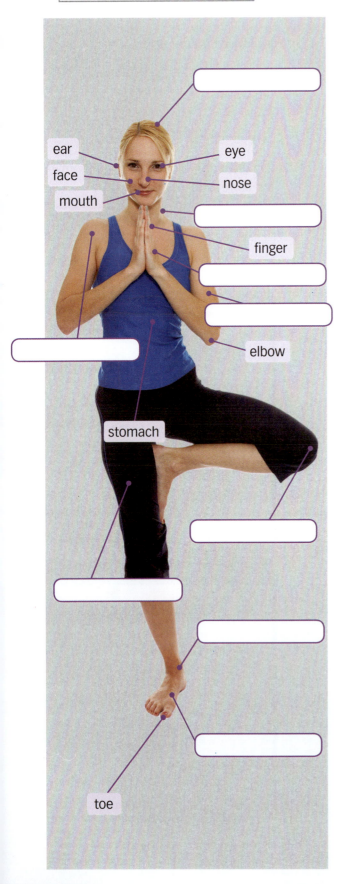

ear, face, mouth, eye, nose, finger, elbow, stomach, toe

Speaking > Benefits of Yoga

1 Work in pairs. Look at the yoga positions and say what parts of the body benefit from them.

2 Work in groups. Draw a new yoga position. Explain what parts of the body benefit from the position.

Reading > Pilates

1 Read the instructions for a Pilates activity and mark (✓) the picture they refer to.

South Bank Pilates Group

Activity #3
Difficulty: Medium
Time required: 5 minutes

Instructions: Lie on your back with your legs on the floor and your arms at your side. Bring your knees up to your chest slowly, legs parallel to the floor. Put your chin to your chest firmly and gradually raise your shoulders off the floor. Then lift your arms steadily and move them up and down quickly. Breathe in slowly and move your arms up and down ten times. Now lower your knees carefully. Don't let your feet fall hard. Relax. Stretch your legs out completely. Lift your hands to the ceiling. Now, raise your head carefully and put your fingers on your toes. Lie back. Repeat the same movements five times.

2 Complete the sentences with parts of the body from the instructions.

a. Bring your _____ up slowly.
b. Raise your _____ off the floor.
c. Lift your _____ steadily.
d. Stretch your _____.

86 Unit 8

Grammar > Adverbs of Manner

1 Work in pairs. Look at the examples from *Track 44* and decide if the underlined adverbs describe actions or things.

> *Bend your left leg gradually.*
> *Move slowly.*
> *Lift your arms steadily.*
> *Don't let your hands fall hard on the floor.*
>
> See *Grammar Reference*, page 108.

2 Match the sentence halves to complete the rules.

a. Adverbs like *hard* and *well*…
b. For most adjectives, …
c. When adjectives end in *-y*, …
d. For adjectives ending in *-l*, …

___ we double the *l* and add *-y*.
___ we replace the *y* with *ily*.
___ we add *-ly*.
___ are irregular.

3 Complete the table with the missing word forms.

Adjective	Adverb
slow	___
patient	___
careful	___
polite	___
___	happily
easy	___
___	well
___	badly

4 Complete the paragraph with the correct form of the words in parentheses.

Jake was late for yoga class. He ran 1) _____ (quick) to the gym. The instructor was already there, so he waited 2) _____ (patient). Then he went into the room 3) _____ (quiet). He lay down on a mat and listened 4) _____ (careful). He was good at yoga and he did the exercises 5) _____ (easy). At the end of the session, he stretched out 6) _____ (complete) and relaxed. That night he slept very 7) _____ (good).

Writing > A Warm-up Routine

1 Use the pictures to write a warm-up routine. Use appropriate adverbs.

2 Work in groups. Take turns reading your routines while the rest of the group does the actions. Give instructions as they do them.

Move slowly, John!
Breathe deeply, Irene!

Out and About

Reading > **SAD**

1. Read the article and write what the acronym SAD represents.

   _____

2. Mark the sentences *T* (true) or *F* (false).

   a. People often have more energy in sunny weather. ___
   b. More than a quarter of people in Canada suffer from SAD. ___
   c. Doctors cannot help people who suffer from SAD. ___
   d. Special lights that imitate daylight help people who suffer from SAD. ___
   e. Rujkan does not get direct sunlight because it is always winter there. ___
   f. The mirrors at Rujkan are in the town square. ___

Vocabulary > **Weather**

> Match the weather to the seasons. Some weather goes with more than one season.

Sunny	Rainy	Snowy
Cloudy	Foggy	Cold
Hot	Wet	Dry	Windy

spring	summer	fall	winter

88   Unit 8

When you are SAD, look in the mirror

The weather affects people in many ways. People often feel more energetic on sunny days. They get tired more quickly when it is cloudy. Some people get headaches in foggy weather and older people often suffer from backaches when it rains. We generally get more colds in winter.

In some parts of the world, long winters with little sunlight cause serious depression problems. One in six Canadians suffers from Seasonal Affective Disorder, or SAD. People with SAD often want to sleep all the time. For SAD sufferers, doctors prescribe simple remedies such as exercise and eating a balanced diet. Some recommend particular vitamins as well, especially vitamin D, which is good for improving mood.

Some people buy special lamps that imitate daylight. A town in Norway has gone even further. Rujkan is surrounded by steep forested hills and does not receive direct sunlight for six months of the year. The authorities decided to put three giant mirrors on top of the hills. The mirrors shine a 600 square meter area of light onto the town square. Now people go there to sit on the benches and enjoy the sun on their faces. Children play. Tourists take pictures. Rujkan is not SAD anymore.

Writing > The Weather

> Choose two cities or regions in your country. Write a short description of the weather in each place.

Listening > *What's the matter?*

1. Match what the people say to the pictures.

    a. I have a backache.
    b. I have a cough.
    c. I have a fever.
    d. I have the flu.
    e. I have a headache.
    f. I have a stomachache.
    g. I have a toothache.
    h. I have an earache.

2. Listen 🎧 to the teens describe how they feel. Underline the symptoms in activity 1 that the boy and the girl have.

3. Listen again and write *S* (Sam) or *A* (Andrea), according to who says each thing.

    a. Go home ___
    b. Take an aspirin ___
    c. Go for a walk ___
    d. Go to the nurse ___

Grammar > Making Suggestions

1 Read the examples from *Track 47* and circle the words that follow the underlined phrases.

> <u>Why don't you</u> go home?
> <u>What about</u> seeing the school nurse?
> <u>How about</u> taking an aspirin?
> <u>Shall we</u> go for a walk?
> <u>Let's</u> go!
>
> See *Grammar Reference*, page 109.

2 Write the underlined phrases in the table.

Expression followed by a gerund (-ing)	Expression followed by base verb

3 Complete the suggestions with the correct form of the verbs in parentheses. Then underline the appropriate response to each.

a. Why don't you _____ (take) an aspirin?
   1. I do, thanks.   2. That's a good idea.

b. Shall we _____ (go) for a bike ride?
   1. Sounds like fun!   2. OK. Have fun!

c. How about _____ (call) the doctor?
   1. No, I'm not.   2. I'll do it now.

d. What about _____ (take) a rest?
   1. Hmm… maybe.   2. They already did.

4 Number the parts of the conversations in the correct order.

Conversation 1

You have to see the dentist. ___
I have a toothache. ___
What's the matter? ___
Ok, but I want you to go with me! ___

Conversation 2

No, I have a stomachache. ___
Are you feeling OK? ___
Yes, that's a good idea. ___
Why don't we call the doctor? ___

Speaking > A Role-play

1 Work in pairs. Use the prompts to prepare a conversation between two friends. Friend 1 makes suggestions to friend 2, who is sick.

Friend 1   Friend 2

- Ask what the matter is.
- Describe your problem.
- Ask for more information.
- Answer the question.
- Make a suggestion.
- Reject the suggestion.
- Make another suggestion.
- Accept the suggestion and say thank you.

2 Act out your conversation for the class.

Review

1 Put the foods into the correct shopping basket.

> orange   pasta   apple   chocolate   carrot
> rice   strawberry   milk   egg   salad

> Add three more words to each basket.

2 Look at the picture and complete the dialogue.

A: Are there 1) _____ apples?
B: Yes, there are 2) _____ apples on the shelf.
A: Is there 3) _____ milk?
B: No, there isn't 4) _____.
A: What about cheese? Is there 5) _____ cheese?
B: Yes, there's 6) _____ cheese.

3 Complete the questions with the correct form of the words in the box.

> careful   quick   polite   slow

a. Do you shower _____ or _____ in the morning?
b. Do you wait _____ in a line?
c. Do you listen _____ to your teacher?
d. Do you ask for things _____?
e. Do you speak English _____?

> Work in pairs. Use the questions to interview each other.

4 Match the questions to the responses.

a. What's the matter?
b. Do you have a fever or a cough?
c. Do you eat healthy food?
d. Why don't you take some vitamin D?
e. What about getting more exercise?

____ No, I don't.
____ I'm not feeling very well.
____ I do lots now, doctor.
____ Yes, I do. I eat a lot of fresh vegetables and fruit.
____ Vitamin D? OK.

5 Read the text and underline the things that you do regularly.

Avoiding Winter Colds

Tip 1: Remember to wash your hands when you meet people with a cold or the flu. Always cover your mouth when you cough.

Tip 2: Get a lot of sleep. Everyone is more open to illness when they are tired, so it is very important to sleep well during the colder months. Seven or eight hours a night are ideal.

Tip 3: Eat well. Eat lots of fresh fruit and vegetables at this time of year.

Tip 4: Keep warm. We get viruses more easily when we are cold. Hide your nose behind a warm scarf in colder weather.

Tip 5: Exercise more not less in cold weather.

> Write a list of tips about staying happy and healthy in the summer.

Student A

Pairwork

Unit 3 (page 40)

Useful Language
In my picture the boy has black jeans.
Her dress is white.

> Work in pairs. Take turns describing the characters' clothes in your picture. Find five differences.

Unit 4 (page 50)

Useful Language
How long does it take to…?
It takes (about)…

1 Ask your partner questions to complete the information.

Travel information — Madison to Franklin

2 Use the information to answer your partner's questions.

Travel information — Riverside to Jackson

	Dep	Arr
🚌	7:15	7:40
🚇	7:55	8:10

🚲 1 and a quarter hours approx.
🚶 3 hours approx.

92 Pairwork

Student A

Unit 5 (page 60)

Useful Language
In my picture, the lion is drinking water.

> Work in pairs. Take turns describing the people and things in your picture to your partner. Find six differences. Then look at your partner's picture to check.

Unit 6 (page 64)

Useful Language
Who was…?
Where was he/she born?
When was he/she born?

1 Look at the table and write questions to ask about Simón Bolívar and Mother Teresa.

	Who?	Where born?	When?	Why famous?	Statue where?
Simón Bolívar					
Mother Teresa					

2 Work in pairs. Ask your partner the questions and complete the table.

3 Read the information about David Livingstone and Joan of Arc. Then answer your partner's questions.

> David Livingstone was a famous explorer and missionary in Africa. He was born in Scotland in 1813. He was the first European to see the Victoria Falls on the River Nile. His statue is in Zambia, near the falls.

> Joan of Arc was born in France in 1412. Joan was only a young girl, but she was a famous soldier and a leader of the French army against the English. There is a statue of Joan in Paris.

Pairwork 93

Student B

Pairwork

Unit 3 (page 40)

Useful Language
In my picture the boy has blue jeans.
Her dress is yellow.

> Work in pairs. Take turns describing the characters' clothes in your picture. Find five differences.

Unit 4 (page 50)

Useful Language
How long does it take to…?
It takes (about)…

1 Use the information to answer your partner's questions.

Travel information — Madison to Franklin

	Dep	Arr		
🚌	3:10	3:55	🚲	2 and a half hours approx.
🚇	3:30	4:00	🚶	6 hours approx.

2 Ask your partner questions to complete the information.

Student B

Unit 5 (page 60)

Useful Language
In my picture, the lion isn't drinking water.
He is sleeping.

> Work in pairs. Take turns describing the people and things in your picture to your partner. Find six differences. Then look at your partner's picture to check.

Unit 6 (page 64)

Useful Language
Who was…?
Where was he/she born?
When was he/she born?

1 Look at the table and write questions to ask about David Livingstone and Joan of Arc.

	Who?	Where born?	When?	Why famous?	Statue where?
David Livingstone					
Joan of Arc					

2 Read the information about Simón Bolívar and Mother Teresa. Then work in pairs and answer your partner's questions.

> Simón Bolívar was a soldier and a political leader. He was born in Caracas in 1783. He was a hero of Latin American independence. There is a statue of Bolívar in Caracas.

> Mother Teresa was a teacher and a missionary in India. She was born in Skopje (now in Macedonia) in 1910. She was famous for helping poor and sick people in Calcutta. There is a statue of Mother Teresa in Skopje.

3 Ask your partner about David Livingstone and Joan of Arc and complete the table.

Project 1 ▾ An English Club

> Interview your classmates.
  a. Do you belong to any clubs or societies? If so, what kind?
  b. Would you like to join a club? Why or why not?
  c. What kinds of clubs are most interesting to you?
  d. What clubs or societies do your friends or family members belong to?

▾ Analyze

- Match the text types to the materials.
  1. A flyer
  2. A membership card
  3. A badge

- Read the texts and answer the questions.
  1. What is the name of the club?
     _____
  2. Is it necessary to register?
     _____
  3. When is the first meeting?
     _____
  4. What resources are there at the club?
     _____

- Find and underline examples of the verb *to be* in the materials.

Grange Hill English Club

Make new friends and learn English! Join our English Club. The English Club meets every Monday in the school library. There are also social activities outside school on Saturdays.

Resources

There are lots of resources at the club. There are two computers with an Internet connection. There is a TV and there are movies in English. There are also books, magazines, and dictionaries in English.

Join now!

Everyone is welcome. Please write your name and e-mail address on this sheet. The first meeting is on Monday at one o'clock in the library. Come along and get your membership card.

▾ Evaluate

- Use the questions to evaluate the materials.
  1. Does the club sound interesting? Why or why not?
  2. Are the materials attractive? If so, what do you like about them? If not, why?
  3. What information would you add to make the materials more attractive?

Contacts

Gloria: glope@hotmail.com

Sami: samih@phone.net

Your name	Your e-mail
1. Susana Díaz	sudi@hotmail.com
2.	
3.	
4.	

- Work in groups. Compare your answers to the questions. Discuss ways to make the club materials better.

Useful Language

I think the materials need more…
There isn't enough…
I like…
… is interesting.

▼ Research

- Work in groups. Create an English Club for students in your school and prepare promotional materials.
- Divide your group into pairs. Assign each pair a topic to research on the Internet about English clubs in other schools: how often clubs meet, what resources they have, what activities they organize, etc.
- With your partner, look for information about your topic.

▼ Prepare

- In your group, discuss the results of your research and decide on the characteristics of your club.
    1. When does the club meet?
    2. Where does the club meet?
    3. What resources does the club have?
    4. What activities does the club organize?
    5. What is the name of your club?
- Divide your group into two and assign tasks.
    1. Designing a badge and a membership card.
    2. Writing and designing a flyer.

▼ Write a First Draft

- Prepare a first draft of your promotional materials.

▼ Edit Your Work

- In your group, evaluate and correct each other's work. Use the questions to guide you.
    1. Is the information clear?
    2. Is the vocabulary appropriate?
    3. Are the grammar and punctuation correct?
    4. Are the materials attractive?

▼ Write a Final Draft

- Write a clean version of your part of the promotional materials.

▼ Create a Final Product

- In your group, collate all the promotional materials.
- Display your group's work on a table for your classmates to see.

▼ Present

- Describe your promotional materials to the class. Highlight the benefits of joining your club.
- Study the information about the different clubs. Choose one to join.
- Register and fill out the membership card for the club you choose.

Projects 97

Project 2 ▾ A Class Presentation

> Work in groups. Discuss the questions.
> a. What do you use to make school presentations? (Posters, computers, etc.)
> b. What do you enjoy about making presentations? What do you not enjoy?

▾ **Analyze**

- Look at the slides of Josie's presentation and underline what it is about.
  1. Favorite Possessions
  2. Favorite Clothes
  3. Favorite Teachers
- Look and number Josie's presentation slides in order.
- Circle the correct words.
  1. We use *bar/pie* graphs to compare items between different groups.
  2. We use *bar/pie* graphs to show results using percentages.

▾ **Evaluate**

- Work in groups. Circle the numbers to evaluate the presentation.

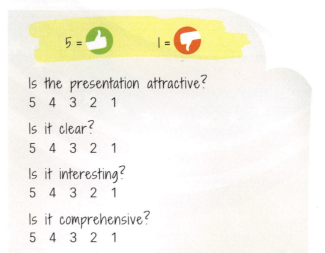

Is the presentation attractive?
5 4 3 2 1

Is it clear?
5 4 3 2 1

Is it interesting?
5 4 3 2 1

Is it comprehensive?
5 4 3 2 1

- Discuss how to improve the presentation.

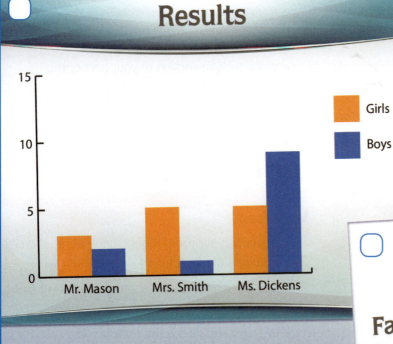

Thank you!

Favorite Teachers Survey

by Josie Cross

98 Projects

Prepare

- Work in groups. You are going to do a Likes and Dislikes Survey and create a presentation of the results. Follow the steps.

  Step 1: Choose a topic (for example, clothes, possessions, or weekend activities).

  Step 2: Write your survey questions.

  Step 3: Ask your teacher or classmates to check your questions.

Do Your Survey

- Work in pairs. Ask people your survey questions and record their answers.

Analyze the Results

- In your group, add all the results together.
- Discuss the results and note your conclusions. For example, hanging out with friends is the favorite activity of teens.

Write a First Draft

- Choose a design for your presentation as a group.
- Assign different sections of the presentation to each pair.
- Write a first draft of your slides.

Edit your Work

- Exchange your work with a different pair. Evaluate and correct their slides. Use the questions as a guide.
  1. Is the spelling and punctuation correct?
  2. Is the vocabulary correct and appropriate?
  3. Is the grammar correct?
  4. Is the information clear?
  5. Is the design appropriate?

Write a Final Draft

- Rewrite your slides to include the corrections.

Create a Final Presentation

- Make any final changes.
- Decide who will present each section.
- Practice giving the presentation. Remember to speak slowly and clearly.

Present

- Make your presentation to the class.

Survey Population

Boys Girls

12   13

Questions
- Who is your favorite teacher?
- Why?

Conclusions

Ms. Dickens

Projects 99

Project 3 — An Exotic Pet Website

Analyze

- Read the introduction on an exotic pets website and identify its mission.
- Complete the animal profile with the questions.
  1. What do they eat?
  2. What do they like doing?
  3. How big do they grow?
  4. Where do they come from?
  5. Are they in danger of extinction?
  6. Are they dangerous?
- Find and underline examples of the language used in the website.
  1. Descriptions of things happening at this moment in time
  2. Expressions of preferences
  3. Expressions of purpose

Evaluate

- Work in pairs. Use the questions to evaluate the materials.
  1. Is the webpage interesting? Why or why not?
  2. What information would you change or add to make the page more interesting?
  3. Is it attractive? If so, what do you like about it? If not, why?
- Work in groups. Compare your answers to the questions. Discuss ways to make the website better.

Research

- Work in groups. Create an Exotic Pet of the Week page for the website. Follow the steps.

  Step 1: Choose an exotic animal to feature on your page. Decide what sections you are going to have.
  - Situation in the Wild
  - Living Conditions
  - Food
  - Habits
  - Dos and Don'ts
  - Gallery
  - Other

  Step 2: Divide your group into pairs. Assign different sections to each pair to research.

  Step 3: In your pair, find information about your section and take notes to include in it.

Prepare

- Compare notes in your group. Make suggestions to each pair about what information to include in the text of their section.

Write a First Draft

- Write a first draft of your section of the page.

Edit Your Work

- In your group, evaluate and correct each other's work. Use the questions to guide you.
  1. Is the information clear?
  2. Is the vocabulary appropriate?
  3. Are the grammar and punctuation correct?

Write a Final Draft

- Write a clean version of your section of the website. Include photos or illustrations.

Create a Final Product

- Collate the information to make the website. Include photos or illustrations.

Present

- Display your work around the classroom.
- Use the questions to evaluate other groups' websites.
  1. How interesting is it?
  2. How attractive is it?
  3. Is the language correct?
- Vote on the best website.

Responsible Exotic Pets

| EXOTIC PETS |
| BIRDS |
| FISH |
| INSECTS |
| **TURTLES** |
| SPIDERS |
| MAMMALS |

Welcome to REP

REP is an exotic pet website that campaigns for owner responsibility. There is a growing trade in illegal exotic pets. Many of these animals are endangered in the wild. It is important to remember this and buy your pet from a legitimate exotic pet store or dealer. Buying from illegal traders is bad for the animal and bad for you. It endangers the species and the animals are often in poor health. Our mission is to protect exotic species in the wild and give information about how to keep exotic pets at home: the food they need, their living conditions, and some dos and don'ts. Click on our animal section, find out about the animal you want to take care of, and see pictures of some happy exotic pet owners. Remember: having an exotic pet is fun but also a big responsibility!

Gordon Brent

Director, REP

Thanks to Irene Salazar for this great pic of her new pets. The baby turtles come from a legitimate pet store and are swimming in their new home!

Mateo Gomez sent us this picture of his turtle, Sheila. Sheila is eating her favorite food.

This is Alicia Garcia's turtle, Gus. Gus is five years old. In this photo, he is climbing on a rock in his enclosure.

KEEPING A SNAPPING TURTLE

- Are they in danger of extinction?
  Yes, in some areas adult and baby snapping turtles are near extinction. Some people collect baby snapping turtles and snapping turtle eggs from the wild to supply pet stores, leading to a population crisis. Be sure you buy one born in captivity.
- _____?
  Snapping turtles can be found in southeastern Canada, western United States, Mexico, and even as far south as Ecuador. They live in freshwater areas.
- _____?
  They grow up to 20 inches in length.
- _____?
  Snapping turtles are usually docile, but be careful when you pick them up—they sometimes hiss and bite!
- _____?
  They enjoy sitting in the sun and exploring.
- _____?
  They love eating meat, vegetables, leaves, grass, and fruit, but eating sugar is bad for them. Turtles also need extra calcium to keep their shells strong.

Here is a list of dos and don'ts:
- Bathe your turtle two or three times a week in warm water.
- Clean its enclosure regularly.
- Give the turtle fresh water every day.
- Don't touch your turtle too much.
- Don't let your dog play with the turtle.
- Don't put oil on the turtle's shell.
Remember to be **RESPONSIBLE!**

Projects 101

Project 4 ▾ A Modern Fable

▾ Analyze

- Read the original version of the fable and complete the analysis.
- Underline examples of the simple past and adjectives in the fable.

▾ Evaluate

- Read the modern version of the fable and answer the questions.
  1. Is the story interesting? Why or why not?
  2. If not, how could you change it to make it more interesting?
  3. Is the comic attractive? If so, what do you like about it? If not, how would you change it?
- Work in groups of four. Compare your answers to the questions. Discuss ways to make the comic better.

The Bundle of Sticks

An old man was on his death bed. He called his sons around him to give them some final advice. He ordered his servants to bring in a bundle of sticks. He said to his eldest son, "Break it."

The son tried and tried, but he could not break the bundle. The other sons also tried, but none of them was successful.

"Untie the bundle," said the father, "and each of you take a stick."

When they each had a stick, he called out to them, "Now, break." Each son broke a stick easily.

"You see," said the father, "Teamwork makes us strong."

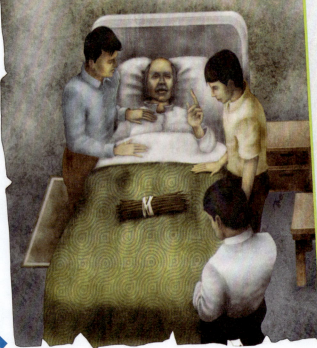

Fable project: Modern version notes

Our modern fable is called "Teamwork wins the day!" We changed the characters to a man named Bill and a group of volunteers. The setting is a town next to a river during a flood. We created a cartoon strip with five illustrations for a story.

Fable Project Analysis

Title: The Bundle of Sticks

Place: Old man's home

Characters: An old man and _____

Main events:

1. An old man asked his sons to break some sticks.
2. The sons could not do it.
3. The old man _____ some advice.
4. _____

Moral of the fable: Teamwork makes us strong.

▼ **Research**
- Work in groups. Find a traditional fable and make notes. Do a Fable Project Analysis like the one on page 88.

▼ **Prepare**
- Follow the steps.

  Step 1: In your group, brainstorm ideas and invent a modern version of the fable.

  Step 2: Decide how many panels your fable will need. Plan illustrations and text for each panel.

  Step 3: Assign each group member a panel to draw.

▼ **Write a First Draft**
- Divide the panels among group members. Each group member writes text for the assigned panel.

▼ **Edit Your Work**
- Exchange panels and correct each other's text. Put all of the panels in order and answer the questions as a group.
  1. Is the story clear?
  2. Do the sketches match the text?
  3. Is the language correct?

▼ **Write a Final Draft**
- Write a final version of your text based on your group members' suggestions.

▼ **Create a Final Product**
- Write notes explaining the modern version of the fable you chose. Arrange your notes and panels so that they are attractive.

▼ **Present**
- Display your fable and the notes around the classroom. Look at other groups' fables. Vote on the best one.

Projects 103

Grammar Reference

Unit 1

Simple Present *to be* (See page 14)

Use

- We use the verb **to be** in the simple present tense to give information about people or things.

Affirmative and Negative

I	am (I'm)	
	am not (I'm not)	
He She It	is (He's/She's/It's) is not (isn't)	from Canada.
We You They	are (We're/You're/They're) are not (aren't)	

Questions

Are they your friends?
Is the girl from Scotland?

Short Answers

Are you a student?	Yes, I am. No I am (I'm) not.
Is he English?	Yes, he is. No, he is not (isn't).
Are they happy?	Yes, they are. No, they are not (aren't).

Imperatives (See page 17)

Use

- We use the imperative for:
  1. rules
  2. warnings
  3. instructions
  4. recipes

Form

Affirmative

Arrive at the station on time.

Negative

Don't run in the hallways.

There is/There are (See page 20)

Use

- We use **there is** and **there are** to introduce a topic or to say that something exists.
  There are computers in the classroom.
  Is there an electronic whiteboard?

Affirmative and Negative

There	is is not (isn't)	a number on the door.
There	are are not (aren't)	two new students in our class.

Unit 2

Simple Present (Affirmative and Negative) (See page 24)

Use

- We use the simple present to indicate:
  1. Something that happens over a long period of time or is a regular, habitual activity.
     I go to school at nine, but Miguel goes at seven.
  2. A permanent situation.
     I live in the US.
  3. A time-tabled event.
     The train leaves at six o'clock.

Form

- The form only changes in third person singular.

Affirmative and Negative

I We You They	go to school at nine. don't go to school at nine.
He She It	goes to school at nine. doesn't go to school at nine.

Simple Present (Questions and Short Answers) (See page 27)

- Questions can begin with question words:
  what, where, which, how, who, when, why, whose.
  What do you do on Sundays?
  Where do you live?
  When do you visit your grandparents?

- The answer to questions without a question word is **yes** or **no**.
  Do you go out on Fridays? Yes, I do./No, I don't.

Questions

Where	do	I we you they	live?
	does	he she it	

Short Answers

Do you go out on Fridays?	Yes, I do. No, I do not (don't).
Does Debbie live close?	Yes, she does. No, she does not (doesn't).

Adverbs of Frequency (See page 30)

never	0% of the time
sometimes	20%–50% of the time
usually, often	60–90% of the time
always	100% of the time

- The position of adverbs of frequency in a sentence depends on which verb is used.
  1. They go before principal verbs.
     *I **always** get up early to help my dad with the animals.*
     *I **usually** walk to school.*
  2. They go after the verb **to be**.
     *There's **often** a baseball game.*

Unit 3

Expressing Likes and Dislikes (See page 34)

Use

- We use **love**, **like**, **don't like**, and **hate** to express likes and dislikes. We follow these verbs with a noun.
  *I **love** Fridays.*
  *I **like** P.E.*
  *I **don't like** Saturdays.*
  *I **hate** Mondays!*

Expressing Likes and Dislikes (3rd Person Singular) (See page 37)

Use

- We can follow **love**, **like**, **doesn't like**, and **hate** with a gerund too.
  *I **love playing** guitar and bass guitar.*
  *She **likes hanging** out with friends.*
  *She **doesn't like shopping**.*
  *We both **hate walking** it.*
- We express likes and dislikes in 3rd person singular by adding –s to the verb. We make negative sentences by using the auxiliary **does not** (**doesn't**) before the verb in the base form.
  *Karen **likes** chatting online.*
  *He **doesn't like** rock.*

Form

Affirmative

He She It	loves likes hates	walking.

Negative

He She It	does not (doesn't)	like	sleeping.

Possessive Adjectives (See page 40)

Use

- We use possessive adjectives to show something belongs to somebody or to express relationship with someone.
  *I like **their** jackets.*
  ***Her** necklace is great.*
  *They are **my** new friends.*

Form

- Each personal pronoun has its own possessive adjective.

Personal Pronouns	Possessive Adjectives
I	my
you	your
he	his
she	her
it	its
we	our
they	their

Grammar Reference

Unit 4

Whose (See page 44)

Use

- We use **whose** to ask who an object belongs to. It can be used as an interrogative pronoun, especially with **be**.
  Whose is this one? That's Lily's.
- It is also an interrogative adjective and is followed by a noun.
  So whose board is it? I don't know.

Form

| Whose | is | this basketball? |
| Whose | are | these shoes? |

| Whose | skateboard | is | this? |
| Whose | sneakers | are | these? |

Possessive Pronouns (See page 44)

Use

- We use possessive pronouns in place of a noun. We use them to refer to possession and belonging.
  Whose is this pen? It's mine.
  Whose is this board? It's hers.
  Whose are these helmets? They're theirs.

Form

- Each personal pronoun has its own possessive pronoun.

Personal Pronouns	Possessive Pronouns
I	mine
You	yours
he	his
she	hers
it	its
we	ours
they	theirs

What/How about + Noun or Gerund (See page 47)

Use

- We use **what/how about** followed by a noun or gerund to make suggestions.
  What about a football? No, I want to buy him something special.
  How about going to the movies? I can't.

Form

| What | about | spaghetti for dinner? |
| How | | a game of cards? |

How long does it take? (See page 50)

Use

- We use **how long** to ask questions about the duration of something. We use **how long does it take** to ask about the time it takes to do something.
  How long does it take? Not long.
  How long does it take to cycle? It takes about two hours.

Form

| How long | does it take | ? |
| | | to go by bus? |

Unit 5

Gerunds (-ing) (See page 54)

Use

- We use the gerund when the verb is the subject of the sentence.
  Feeding him is the easy part.
- We use the gerund when the verb comes after a preposition.
  How about getting an iguana?
- We use the gerund after verbs of preference such as **enjoy, like, love, hate**.
  He loves climbing up my arm.
  He enjoys hiding in his cage.

Infinitives (Purpose) (See page 57)

Use

- We use the infinitive with **to** to show purpose.
  Foxes visit people's yards to eat pet food.
  They move quietly to avoid detection.
  They watch the animal closely to see if there is danger.

Present Continuous (See page 60)

Use

- We use the present continuous to describe an action that is happening around this moment in time.
  The zebras are arriving now.

Form

- We form the present continuous tense with the verb **to be** + the present participle (-ing).

- **Affirmative and Negative**

I	am (I'm)	
	am not (I'm not)	
He	is (He's/She's/It's)	looking
She		around.
It	is not (isn't)	
We	are (We're/You're/They're)	
You		
They	are not (aren't)	

Questions

What	am	I	doing?
	is	he	
		she	
		it	
	are	we	
		you	
		they	

Short Answers

Are you taking pictures of the animals?	Yes, I am.
	No, I am (I'm) not.
Is the zebra looking around?	Yes, it is.
	No, it is not (isn't).

Unit 6

To be (Simple Past and Past Continuous) (See page 64)

Simple Past

Use

- We use the verb **to be** in the simple past to give information about people or things and describe situations that started and finished at a certain moment in the past.

Affirmative and Negative

I	was	
He	was not (wasn't)	
She		at home.
It		
We	were	
You	were not (weren't)	
They		

Questions

Who **was** the sculptor?
Was he American?
Were there any accidents?

Short Answers

Was he American?	Yes, he was.
	No, he was not (wasn't).
Were there any accidents?	Yes, there were.
	No, there were not (weren't).

Simple Past (Regular Verbs) (See page 67)

- We use the simple past to indicate:
  1. An action that is now finished.
     Albert Einstein studied at a secondary school in Munich.
  2. A sequence of events in the past
     Einstein finished high school in Switzerland and entered a science school.

Form

- The form of the simple past is the same for all persons.
  1. The normal rule is to add **-ed** to the base form of the verb.
     finish–finished
  2. We add **-d** to the base form of verbs ending in **e**.
     decide–decided
  3. We eliminate the **y** and add **-ied** to the base form of verbs ending in a consonant + y.
     study–studied
  4. We double the consonant and add **-ed** to verbs ending in a single vowel + consonant.
     stop–stopped

Affirmative

I	
He/She/It	
We	decided to stop buying British products.
You	
They	

Grammar Reference 107

Grammar Reference

Simple Past (Negative, Questions, and Short Answers) (See page 70)

Negative

Use

- We use the auxiliary verb **did not** (**didn't**) before regular and irregular verbs in the base form to form the negative in the simple past tense.

I He/She/It We You They	did not (didn't) start in Boston.

Questions

- We use the auxiliary verb **did** in questions in the simple past tense. The main verb always stays in the base form.

Where did	I he/she/it we you they	start?

Short Answers

Did you hear the question?	Yes, I did. No, I did not (didn't).
Did it start in 1775?	Yes, it did. No, it did not (didn't).

Past Continuous

Use

- We use the past continuous tense to show longer actions in the past. It shows actions that have duration.
- *She was standing in front of the theatre.*

Form

- We form the past continuous tense with the auxiliary **was/were** + the present participle.

Affirmative and Negative

I He She It	was was not (wasn't)	waiting for the doctor.
We You They	were were not (weren't)	

Questions

What	was	I he she it	doing yesterday?
	were	we you they	

Short Answers

Were you waiting for the doctor?	Yes, I was. No, I was not (wasn't)
Was he waiting for the doctor?	Yes, he was. No, he was not (wasn't).
Were you/they waiting for the doctor?	Yes, we/they were. No, we/they were not (weren't).

Unit 7

Relative Clauses (*Who*, *That*, *Where*) (See page 74)

Use

- We can use the pronouns **who**, **that**, and **where** to join two separate sentences.
  1. We use **who** for people.
     Bella is a shy girl. She moves to a new school.
     *Bella is a shy girl, **who** moves to a new school.*
  2. We use **where** for places.
     She moves to a new school. She meets a boy there.
     *She moves to a new school, **where** she meets a boy.*
  3. We use **that** for things or people.
     Edward is a vampire. He drinks animal blood.
     *Edward is a vampire **that** drinks animal blood.*

Simple Past (Irregular Verbs) (See page 77)

There are many irregular verbs. (See page 111)

Past Time Clauses with *When* (See page 80)

Use

We use the simple past with **when** to talk about two consecutive actions in the past. We place **when** before the action that happened first.

The people of the tribe danced and sang **when** *they heard the news.*
When *the boy was two years old his parents decided to go on a trip.*

Unit 8

Countable and Uncountable Nouns (*Some/Any*) (See page 84)

Use

- Countable nouns refer to people, places, and things that you can count and that have plural forms.
  eggs, chips, tomatoes, people
  Uncountable nouns refer to concrete or abstract things that you cannot count. They have no plural forms.
  water, air, intelligence, pasta, broccoli

Some/Any

- **Some** and **any** are used when the speaker cannot specify or does not need or want to specify a number or an exact amount. We use **any** in questions and negative sentences.
  Is there **any** *lemonade on the list?*
  There aren't **any** *chips on Mom's list.*

  We use **some** in affirmative statements.
  There is **some** *pasta.*
  There are **some** *eggs.*

  We can also use **some** in questions when offering or requesting.
  Would you like **some** *more coffee?*
  Could I have **some** *milk, please?*

Adverbs of Manner (See page 87)

Use

- We use adverbs of manner to describe the way in which an action is carried out.

  Bend your left leg **gradually**.
  Move **slowly**.
  Lift your arms **steadily**.
  Don't let your hands fall **hard** *on the floor.*

Form

- We form most adverbs by taking the adjective and adding **-ly**.
  gradual–gradually
  slow–slowly

- When the adjective ends in **y**, we take away the **y** and add **-ily**
  steady–steadily
  happy–happily

- When the adjective ends in a consonant followed by **le**, replace the final **e** with **-y**.
  terrible–terribly, comfortable–comfortably

- Exceptions:
  hard–hard, good–well, fast–fast

Making Suggestions (See page 90)

Use

We use **Why don't...? What about...? How about...? Shall...?** and **Let's** to make suggestions.

Why don't you go home?
What about seeing the school nurse?
How about taking an aspirin?
Shall we go for a walk?
Let's go!

Form

- We use **Why don't...? / Why doesn't...?** followed by the base form of the verb.
  Why don't I/you/we/they pick them up at eight?
  Why doesn't he/she take a rest.

- We follow **How about...?** and **What about..?** with a gerund or a noun.
  How about going to the school nurse?
  What about taking an aspirin?
  How about tomorrow at noon?

- We use **Shall...?** with **I** and **we** followed by the base form of the verb.
  Shall we sit down?
  Shall I open a window?

Phonetic Symbols

Consonant sounds		
/p/	as in	pet /pɛt/
/b/	as in	bat /bæt/
/t/	as in	tip /tɪp/
/d/	as in	dig /dɪg/
/k/	as in	cat /kæt/
/g/	as in	good /gʊd/
/f/	as in	fit /fɪt/
/v/	as in	van /væn/
/s/	as in	sip /sɪp/
/z/	as in	zip /zɪp/
/l/	as in	lid /lɪd/
/m/	as in	mat /mæt/
/n/	as in	nine /naɪn/
/h/	as in	hat /hæt/
/r/	as in	rat /ræt/
/j/	as in	yes /jɛs/
/w/	as in	win /wɪn/
/θ/	as in	thin /θɪn/
/ð/	as in	the /ðə/
/ʃ/	as in	ship /ʃɪp/
/ʒ/	as in	vision /ˈvɪʒən/
/tʃ/	as in	chin /tʃɪn/
/dʒ/	as in	Japan /dʒəˈpæn/
/ŋ/	as in	English /ˈɪŋglɪʃ/

Vowel sounds		
/i/	as in	very /vɛri/
/i:/	as in	see /si:/
/ɪ/	as in	bit /bɪt/
/ɛ/	as in	ten /tɛn/
/æ/	as in	stamp /stæmp/
/ɑ/	as in	father /ˈfɑðər/
/o/	as in	sore /sor/
/ʊ/	as in	book /bʊk/
/u:/	as in	you /ju:/
/ʌ/	as in	sun /sʌn/
/ə/	as in	about /əˈbaʊt/
/ɑ:/	as in	dog /dɑ:g/
/eɪ/	as in	fate /feɪt/
/aɪ/	as in	fine /faɪn/
/ɔɪ/	as in	boy /bɔɪ/
/aʊ/	as in	now /naʊ/
/oʊ/	as in	go /goʊ/
/ɪə/	as in	near /nɪər/
/eə/	as in	hair /heər/

Irregular Verbs

Base form	Simple past	Past participle
be	was/were	been
become	became	become
begin	began	begun
break	broke	broken
bring	brought	brought
build	built	built
buy	bought	bought
catch	caught	caught
choose	chose	chosen
come	came	come
cost	cost	cost
do	did	done
drink	drank	drunk
drive	drove	driven
eat	ate	eaten
fall	fell	fallen
feel	felt	felt
fight	fought	fought
find	found	found
fly	flew	flown
forget	forgot	forgotten
get	got	gotten
give	gave	given
go	went	gone
grow	grew	grown
have	had	had
hear	heard	heard
hit	hit	hit
keep	kept	kept
know	knew	known

Base form	Simple past	Past participle
leave	left	left
lose	lost	lost
make	made	made
meet	met	met
pay	paid	paid
put	put	put
read /ri:d/	read /red/	read /red/
ride	rode	ridden
run	ran	run
say	said	said
see	saw	seen
sell	sold	sold
send	sent	sent
shut	shut	shut
sing	sang	sung
sit	sat	sat
sleep	slept	slept
speak	spoke	spoken
spend	spent	spent
steal	stole	stolen
swim	swam	swum
take	took	taken
tell	told	told
think	thought	thought
throw	threw	thrown
understand	understood	understood
wake	woke	woken
wear	wore	worn
win	won	won
write	wrote	written

Workbook Unit 1

1 Circle the eight nationalities.

```
H  M  C  G  I  Z  O  F  W  I  J  P
K  W  H  L  T  N  O  B  R  R  L  Z
B  N  I  J  A  H  U  S  A  I  Z  J
R  U  N  E  L  V  F  I  I  S  J  I
A  M  E  R  I  C  A  N  U  H  Y  P
Z  U  S  Q  A  I  J  D  W  L  F  O
I  Q  E  Z  N  L  L  I  Q  S  B  L
L  F  I  G  E  O  O  A  O  V  Z  R
I  H  G  R  E  E  K  N  N  T  D  T
A  N  E  N  G  L  I  S  H  Z  U  A
N  S  O  T  A  X  S  Z  O  L  Q  Y
T  T  C  B  J  X  X  V  Q  I  W  X
```

2 Complete the dialogue with the prompts in parentheses.

DAVID: I'm David. 1) _____ (what/name)?

LAURA: Laura. 2) _____ (you/Spanish)?

DAVID: 3) _____ (No, Peru). Where are you from?

LAURA: The US. 4) _____ (you/a new student)?

DAVID: Yes, I am. Are you a new student?

LAURA: No. 5) _____ (How old…)?

DAVID: 6) _____ (I/15).

LAURA: Me too. 7) _____ (We/the same age).

3 Rewrite the sentences in the negative form.

> He is my brother.
> He isn't my brother.

a. I am from Canada.

_____

b. It's time for lunch.

_____

c. You are in my class.

_____

d. We are from Argentina.

_____

e. They are Moroccan.

_____

f. She is a French teacher.

_____

Workbook Unit 1

4 Use the prompts to write sentences.

> he / not / my cousin
> He isn't my cousin.

a. my friend Yao / Chinese

_____

b. I / not / a teacher

_____

c. I / a student

_____

d. where / you / from?

_____

e. my sister / sixteen and my brother / fourteen

_____

f. what / your phone number?

_____

g. they / new students

_____

5 Match the class rules to the pictures.

◯  ◯

◯  ◯

a. Arrive on time. Three tardies equal one absence.
b. Be prepared. Bring your schoolbooks, notebooks, and pens every day.
c. Bring gym clothes for P.E.
d. Do not eat food in the classroom. There is a cafeteria for snacks.

Workbook Unit 1

6 Unscramble the prompts to write some rules.

a. the books / write / don't / in
_____

b. litter / put / garbage can / in the
_____

c. protective / goggles / wear
_____

d. noise / don't / make / and / quiet / keep
_____

e. the restroom / in / hands / wash / your
_____

7 Match the rules from activity 6 to the places below.

____ classroom   ____ cafeteria   ____ library

____ restroom   ____ laboratory

8 Circle the word that does not belong in each group.

a. pen	pencil	marker	eraser
b. whiteboard	tablet	book	calculator
c. heavy	big	paper	easy
d. reading	student	listening	writing
e. projects	exercises	games	snacks
f. table	desk	chair	school bag

9 Look at the picture. Write questions and answers with the prompts.

> a poster on the wall?
> Is there a poster on the wall? Yes, there is.

a. a shelf for the books?
_____

b. computers for the students?
_____

c. how many desks?
_____

d. an electronic whiteboard?
_____

⌄ Self-Assessment　　　　　　　　　　　　　Unit 1

Think about Unit 1. Write your impressions about each section of the unit. Include what you learned and how you improved.

Unit Opener

_____
_____
_____
_____
_____
_____

My World

_____
_____
_____
_____
_____
_____

Views

_____
_____
_____
_____
_____
_____

Out and About

_____
_____
_____
_____
_____
_____

⌄ What do I have to do to learn more?

☐ Pay more attention in class.　　　　☐ Do more practice exercises.

☐ Participate more in class.　　　　　☐ Study more at home.

☐ Read and listen to English in my free time.　　☐ Practice writing and speaking.

☐ Other: _____

Unit 1　115

Workbook Unit 2

1 Match the phrases to the pictures.

> have lunch   take a shower   go to school   do homework   go to bed   watch TV
> finish school   get up   have breakfast

 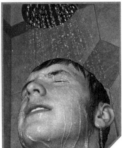  

_____   _____   _____   _____

_____   _____   _____   _____   _____

2 Underline the correct options to complete the sentences.

a. I *live/lives* in San Francisco.

b. You *don't live/doesn't live* in the US.

c. Emily *like/likes* her school.

d. Emily's mother doesn't *work/works* in a hospital.

e. We *has/have* lunch at school.

f. They *go/goes* home at three o'clock.

3 Read the exchange and complete the rules.

> A: *Do you do sports on weekends?*
> B: *Yes, I do.*
> A: *What sport do you do?*
> B: *I play tennis.*
> A: *Does your sister play, too?*
> B: *No, she doesn't. She's a cheerleader for the football team.*

a. We use the auxiliary verb _____ to form questions in the simple present.

b. We use _____ for *I, we, you, they* and _____ for *he, she, it*.

c. We also use _____ , _____ , _____ and _____ in short answers.

Workbook Unit 2

4 Use the prompts to write sentences.

a. Susan / get up / 8:20

b. Charlie / ride / a horse / to school

c. Jim / have / a cheese sandwich for lunch

d. Charlie / not play / football

e. Susan and Jim / dance / very well

f. they / not go / to bed late

5 Use the prompts to write questions.

a. you / see your best friend on the weekend?

b. where / live?

c. he / she fun to be with?

d. you / eat lunch with your parents on Sundays?

e. your parents strict?

f. what / your parents do on Sunday afternoons?

g. what time / you go to bed on Sunday evenings?

6 Unscramble the words to form questions.

a. have / breakfast? / you / a / big / Do

b. do / bed? / you / go / to / What / time

c. teachers / uniform? / Do / your / a / wear

d. When / do / go / to / you / movies? / the

e. he / computer games / play / Saturday? / on / Does

Workbook Unit 2

f. do / friends? / meet / you / Where / your
_____

g. comic books / bed? / Does / she / in / read
_____

h. you / your / visit / on / Sunday? / grandparents / Do
_____

7 Connect the questions to the answers.

When do you do your homework?   Yes, I do. I love reading.

Do you go on your computer?   Soccer and ice hockey.

What type of books do you read?   On Saturday mornings if I don't play football with my friends.

Do you go to the library?   No, I don't. I visit them on Sunday.

What sports do you play?   Yes, I do. I go on Facebook and watch videos on YouTube.

Do you visit your family on Saturday? Science fiction and fantasy.

8 Use the adverbs to rewrite the sentences.

a. My father has a cup of coffee for breakfast. (usually)
_____

b. We have dinner before eight o'clock. (always)
_____

c. I'm late for school. (never)
_____

d. I do my homework in the school library. (sometimes)
_____

e. We eat in a restaurant during the week. (rarely)
_____

9 Use the phrases to complete the sentences.

| once a week | three times a day | three times a year | every day | once a year | twice a day |

a. Frank goes shopping on Friday.
_____

b. He brushes his teeth after breakfast, after lunch, and after dinner.
_____

c. He watches TV on Monday, Tuesday, Wednesday, Thursday, Friday, Saturday, and Sunday.
_____

d. His father walks Brandy, their dog, before he goes to work and after he gets home.
_____

e. His parents go to the theater at Christmas.
_____

f. They have vacations in December, in April, and in August.
_____

▾ Self-Assessment   Unit 2

Think about Unit 2. Write your impressions about each section of the unit. Include what you learned and how you improved.

Unit Opener

_____
_____
_____
_____
_____
_____

My World

_____
_____
_____
_____
_____
_____

Views

_____
_____
_____
_____
_____
_____

Out and About

_____
_____
_____
_____
_____
_____

▾ What do I have to do to learn more?

◯ Pay more attention in class.   ◯ Do more practice exercises.

◯ Participate more in class.   ◯ Study more at home.

◯ Read and listen to English in my free time.   ◯ Practice writing and speaking.

◯ Other: _____

Workbook Unit 3

1 Unscramble the sentences.

a. math. / love / I
_____

b. don't / I / history. / like
_____

c. the / we / like / teacher. / don't / science
_____

d. love / geography / they / English. / and
_____

e. English. / students / love / twelve
_____

2 Look at the images and complete the sentences with a verb.

a. I ♥ English. It's fun.
_____

b. We 👎 history. It's boring!
_____

c. They 👍 soccer, but they 👎 basketball.
_____

d. We ♥ Miss White. She's our favorite teacher!
_____

e. I 👍 Fridays, and I ♥ Saturdays.
_____

f. I 😠 math, but I ♥ science.
_____

3 Write sentences about you.

a. (love) _____

b. (like) _____

c. (don't like) _____

d. (hate) _____

Workbook Unit 3

4 Complete the sentences with the correct answer.

| reading | solving | playing | shopping | playing | doing | playing | listening | hanging |

a. Hanna loves _____ sports. She is on the school basketball team.

b. My brother likes _____ guitar in his bedroom. It is electric and it's very noisy!

c. Kevin loves _____ to music.

d. _____ homework is OK. I like _____ math problems.

e. I'm a very social person. I love _____ out with friends.

f. My brother loves _____ books: *Harry Potter* and *The Hunger Games* are his favorites.

g. Going _____ is boring. My mother buys my clothes for me.

h. My favorite hobby is _____ video games.

5 Classify the sentences.

a. Affirmative sentences – verb + -s

b. Negative sentences – *doesn't* + verb without -s

____ He doesn't like singing.

____ Jenny likes rock music.

____ John hates sports.

____ She doesn't hate football!

____ She likes playing the piano.

____ Billy doesn't like Mondays.

6 Underline the correct form.

My best friend James and I are a little different. We both *love/loves* sports but he *like/likes* playing soccer and I *like/likes* playing tennis. I *don't/doesn't* like video games but James *love/loves* video games. We both *like/likes* music. I *love/loves* rock and heavy metal but James *don't/doesn't* like it. He *like/likes* singers like John Legend and Adele. He *love/loves* going shopping but I think it's very boring!

7 Look at the table and complete the sentences.

	Kiera	Ryan
play sports	✗	✓✓
go shopping	✓✓	✗✗
hang out with friends	✓	✓
video games	✗✗	✓✓
listen to music	✓	✗

a. Kiera _____ playing sports.

b. She **loves** _____ going shopping.

c. She _____ listening to music.

d. Ryan _____ going shopping.

e. He _____ hanging out with friends.

f. He _____ listening to music.

Workbook Unit 3

8 Find ten clothing words.

B	A	U	O	T	K	Y	L	F	J	M
A	W	B	S	D	V	F	G	Q	X	C
F	J	E	A	N	S	O	H	M	U	J
G	K	L	R	T	H	P	A	N	T	S
I	E	T	B	B	I	G	T	L	K	H
D	A	U	O	T	R	D	S	X	W	O
R	Q	I	O	Q	T	B	R	P	O	R
E	S	P	T	F	H	J	L	K	T	T
S	X	G	S	N	E	A	K	E	R	S
S	K	A	Q	T	L	B	E	Q	J	S
Q	C	H	Z	A	Q	V	B	Y	B	M
D	S	X	W	T	K	Y	L	U	B	X
K	H	N	E	C	K	L	A	C	E	W
S	B	O	A	K	Y	U	T	L	B	N

9 Complete the sentences with the appropriate possessive adjectives.

> your   his   my   their   our   her

a. I love playing tennis. This is _____ favorite racket.

b. Emily is an actress. She's American and _____ last name is Blunt.

c. — Who is _____ favorite soccer player?
— My favorite soccer player is Neymar.

d. Kate and Naomi are models. They're British and _____ favorite sport is swimming.

e. Carlos and I love playing sports. _____ favorite sport is baseball.

f. I like his jeans but I don't like _____ T-shirt.

10 Write the correct possessive adjective to complete each sentence.

a. Carlos and I love basketball. _____ favorite team is Golden State Warriors.

b. I don't like _____ school uniform. It's very uncool.

c. I like _____ dress. You look great!

d. My friend Steve loves music. _____ favorite possession is his violin.

e. They are in the same school. _____ school has two soccer fields and a basketball court.

f. Erica loves movies. _____ favorite actor is Matt Damon.

⌄ Self-Assessment — Unit 3

Think about Unit 3. Write your impressions about each section of the unit. Include what you learned and how you improved.

Unit Opener

_____
_____
_____
_____
_____
_____
_____

My World

_____
_____
_____
_____
_____
_____
_____

Views

_____
_____
_____
_____
_____
_____

Out and About

_____
_____
_____
_____
_____
_____
_____

⌄ What do I have to do to learn more?

- ☐ Pay more attention in class.
- ☐ Do more practice exercises.
- ☐ Participate more in class.
- ☐ Study more at home.
- ☐ Read and listen to English in my free time.
- ☐ Practice writing and speaking.
- ☐ Other: _____

Workbook Unit 4

1 Use the words to complete the sentences.

> flips   grind   helmet   trick   skateboard   pads

a. The best place to do _____ and grinds is a skateboard park.
b. You wear a _____ to protect your head when you skateboard.
c. I need to fix the wheels of my _____. It's very slow.
d. I'm learning a new _____. It's called the kickflip.
e. If you don't wear _____, you can hurt your elbows or knees.
f. The _____ is a trick where the skateboarder slides along on the truck of the skateboard.

2 Underline the correct words.

a. A: Is this your board?
   B: No, it isn't. *Mine/Yours* is black.
b. A: Whose helmet is this?
   B: I think it's *ours/hers*. She's not wearing one.
c. A: Jim, are these sunglasses *his/yours*?
   B: Yes, thanks. I thought they were lost!
d. This isn't Paolo's phone. *His/Ours* has a big screen.
e. A: Did Annie and Louis leave their pads again?
   B: Yes, those pads are *mine/theirs*.
f. Excuse me. We think this isn't your suitcase. It's *ours/yours*.

3 Use the prompts to write questions.

a. A: _____ (keys)
   B: They're my brother's.
b. A: _____ (camera)
   B: It's mine. I'm in charge of taking the pictures.
c. A: _____ (gloves)
   B: They're Chris'. He needs to protect his hands.
d. A: _____ (uniform)
   B: It's Luciane's! She left it here yesterday.

4 Rewrite the sentences using possessive pronouns.

a. These aren't my shoes.
   _____
b. This is Sarah's board.
   _____
c. Are these Jack's pads?
   _____
d. This isn't our dog.
   _____
e. Are they your boots?
   _____
f. Is this your glass?
   _____

124   Unit 4

Workbook Unit 4

5 Label the feelings.

a. Hey, that's a great idea! I love it!
b. What? You're joking!
c. Oh no!

___ surprised   ___ enthusiastic   ___ worried

6 Complete the table.

Ordinal Numbers	Ordinal Numerals
11	
	twenty-second
43	
	sixty-seventh
72	
	eighty-ninth

7 Match the parts of the conversations.

a. How about going to the park?
b. I'm hungry. What about a pizza?
c. How about giving Alice a gift voucher for her birthday?
d. I'm really bored. What about watching a movie?
e. It's hot. How about some ice cream?
f. I don't understand this math problem.

___ No, that's a boring present.
___ What about asking your teacher for help?
___ Cool! I have some in the fridge. Do you like vanilla?
___ Great idea! Let's buy the tickets online.
___ No, I think it's going to rain.
___ Good idea! I'm really hungry, too.

8 Write suggestions.

a. A: _____
   B: That's a good idea. I'll take my surfboard.

b. A: _____
   B: I can't. I have a lot of homework.

c. A: I'm a bit nervous about the exam.
   B: _____

d. A: _____
   B: No, they're very expensive.

e. A: _____
   B: No, not again. Let's order a pizza.

Workbook Unit 4

9 Solve the crossword.

Across ➔
4. Something that is _____ is highly valued and important.
5. This area isn't very noisy. It's _____.
6. The picture is full of color. It's really _____.

Down ↓
1. It is very unusual or strange. It is _____.
2. Soccer is the most _____ sport. Children and adults play it.
3. Something that is very attractive is _____.

10 Use the words to complete the exchange.

| takes   How   It   long   take   to |

A: Excuse me. How long does it take to go (1) _____ the airport?

B: It (2) _____ about 45 minutes.

A: We want to go shopping. How (3) _____ does it (4) _____ to get to the shopping mall?

B: It's not very far. (5) _____ takes about 20 minutes.

A: What about museums? Are there any interesting museums?

B: Yes, there's the National Museum.

A: Is it far from here? (6) _____ long does it take to get there?

B: About half an hour but you can take a bus and it'll be only ten minutes.

11 Complete the conversations.

a. A: _____ _____ does it take to walk to the park?
   B: _____ takes about half an hour.

b. A: How long _____ _____ _____ from here to the town center?
   B: It takes _____ twenty minutes by bus.

c. A: _____ _____ _____ _____ _____ to drive to the library?
   B: _____ _____ about ten minutes.

d. A: _____ _____ _____ _____ _____ from Scarsdale to New York City by car?
   B: _____ _____ _____ forty-five minutes.

e. A: _____ _____ _____ _____ _____ to get to the nearest hospital?
   B: _____ _____ about ten minutes by car.

▼ Self-Assessment — Unit 4

Think about Unit 4. Write your impressions about each section of the unit. Include what you learned and how you improved.

Unit Opener
_____
_____
_____
_____
_____
_____

My World
_____
_____
_____
_____
_____
_____

Views
_____
_____
_____
_____
_____
_____

Out and About
_____
_____
_____
_____
_____
_____

▼ What do I have to do to learn more?

- ☐ Pay more attention in class.
- ☐ Do more practice exercises.
- ☐ Participate more in class.
- ☐ Study more at home.
- ☐ Read and listen to English in my free time.
- ☐ Practice writing and speaking.
- ☐ Other: _____

Workbook Unit 5

1 Look at the pictures and use the prompts to write sentences about the pets.

| play with the neighbor's cat   wag tail   sleep in her bed   scratch the scratcher   climb trees   bark at strangers |

_____   _____   _____

_____   _____   _____

2 Write a short paragraph about your pet or a friend's pet. Describe the animal's routine and behavior.
   _____
   _____

3 Use the prompts to write sentences.

   a. not like / Most people / touch / spiders
      _____

   b. Birds / fly / enjoy / outside / cages / their
      _____

   c. not like / Many dogs / hugged / be
      _____

   d. love / Cats / birds / catch
      _____

4 Complete the conversation with the correct form of the verbs in parentheses.

   DALE: How about 1) _____ (buy) Ann a book?
   BECKY: No, she doesn't read much. Let's 2) _____ (get) her a DVD.
   DALE: No, she watches movies on the Internet.
   BECKY: Mmm, this is difficult.
   DALE: Yes, the hard part about birthdays is 3) _____ (find) the right gift. How about 4) _____ (try) the clothes boutique?
   BECKY: No, it's too expensive. Let's 5) _____ (look) in the pet store.
   DALE: Not a good idea! Not everyone loves 6) _____ (have) pets.
   BECKY: You're right!

128 Unit 5

Workbook Unit 5

5 Classify the sentences under the correct heading.

(a) Gerund as a subject   (b) Gerund for suggestions

- How about buying a small dog? ____
- Looking after it can be fun. ____
- Feeling lonely is her problem. ____
- Cleaning them is not a problem. ____
- Feeding them is easy. ____
- How about getting a cat? ____

6 Complete the sentences with the correct form of the words in the box.

| keep | take | climb | hunt | build | catch | play | find |

a. Bears _____ in rivers _____ fish.
b. Birds _____ nests in trees _____ their young safe.
c. People _____ their pets to parks _____ with them.
d. Squirrels _____ trees _____ acorns.

7 Read the animal profile and answer the questions.

Brown Rat (Sewer Rat)

- Life span: 4 years
- Size: body: 25 cm; tail: 25 cm
- Weight: 1/2 kg to 3/4 kg

The brown rat or "sewer rat" lives where there are a lot of people. It moves around big cities to get food. The rat digs holes (burrows) in the ground or in buildings to stay safe from predators. It also uses the burrows to store food. Rats form groups to establish a social order. The group members mate each other and live together. They also sleep together to stay warm. Brown rats usually look for food at night to avoid detection. They use ultrasonic sounds and chirping to communicate. Rats also carry disease and reproduce quickly. This is why city governments work hard to keep these urban pests under control.

a. Why do rats dig burrows?
_____
_____
_____

b. Why do they form groups?
_____
_____
_____

c. Why do rats look for food at night?
_____
_____
_____

d. Why do big cities try to control rat populations?
_____
_____
_____

Workbook Unit 5

8 Observe where the adverb is placed in the examples. Then, unscramble the words to form sentences.

> 1. *Foxes run quickly to catch mice and rabbits.*
> 2. *They move quietly to avoid detection.*
> 3. *They watch the animal carefully, and then they attack suddenly.*

a. I / to correct / carefully / my / mistakes. / composition/ read
___

b. and then / went / to play / my / homework / I finished / quickly / video game. / my new
___

c. slowly / caught / The / the lion / ran / it. / so / old zebra
___

d. and / badly / very / lost / I / played / the game.
___

e. a walk. / loudly / for / dog / to go / he wants / barks / when / My
___

9 Use prepositions to answer the questions about your bedroom.

a. Where is your bed?
___

b. Do you have a desk? Where is it?
___

c. Are there any posters in your bedroom? Where are they?
___

d. Where are your clothes?
___

e. Where is the door?
___

f. Is there a chair in your bedroom? Where is it?
___

10 Use the correct form of the verbs to describe what is happening outside the girl's window at the moment of speaking.

| cross | eat | listen | look | paint | play | read | ride | wait | walk | wear |

This is what I can see from the window of my bedroom. Some children 1)_____ in the park. An old lady 2)_____ the road. A girl 3)_____ an ice cream and a man 4)_____ a bicycle. He 5)_____ also _____ to music. Two men 6)_____ a wall. A man 7)_____ his dog. He 8)_____ a funny hat. A man and a woman 9)_____ for the bus. The man 10)_____ the newspaper and the woman 11)_____ at her watch. I'm looking out the window and trying to do my English homework!

⌄ Self-Assessment   Unit 5

Think about Unit 5. Write your impressions about each section of the unit.
Include what you learned and how you improved.

Unit Opener

My World

Views

Out and About

⌄ What do I have to do to learn more?

☐ Pay more attention in class.   ☐ Do more practice exercises.

☐ Participate more in class.   ☐ Study more at home.

☐ Read and listen to English in my free time.   ☐ Practice writing and speaking.

☐ Other: _____

Workbook Unit 6

1 Match the events to the years.

a. The Civil War between the North and the South started in eighteen sixty-one.

b. Buzz Aldrin and Neil Armstrong walked on the Moon in nineteen sixty-nine.

c. Lee Harvey Oswald assassinated President John F. Kennedy in nineteen sixty-three.

d. British colonists founded the Jamestown settlement in sixteen oh-seven.

e. The American colonies wrote the Declaration of Independence in seventeen seventy-six.

f. Christopher Columbus discovered America in fourteen ninety-two.

g. The Great Depression started with the crash of the Stock Market in nineteen twenty-nine.

h. D-Day took place in nineteen forty-four. Allied troops won a major victory in World War II.

___ 1963 ___ 1492 ___ 1861 ___ 1776 ___ 1944 ___ 1929 ___ 1969 ___ 1607

2 Read the examples and complete the table.

> A: Where were you last week?
> B: I was on vacation. I was in San Francisco.
> A: Were your parents with you?
> B: No they weren't. I was there with my aunt and my cousins.
> A: Was it cold?
> B: No, it wasn't. It was pretty warm.

Simple Past *to be*

Affirmative	Negative	Questions	Short answers
I _____	I _____	Was I?	Yes, I _____. No, I _____.
you/we/they _____	you/we/they _____	Were you/we/they?	Yes, you/we/they _____. No, you/we/they _____.
he/she/it _____	he/she/it _____	Was he/she/it?	Yes, he/she/it _____. No, he/she/it _____.

3 Complete the text with the correct form of the verb *to be*.

The 1.7-mile-long Golden Gate Bridge across San Francisco Bay is a technical masterpiece.

When workers completed the bridge in 1937, it 1) _____ the tallest and longest suspension bridge in the world.

The designer 2) _____ the engineer Joseph Strauss. At first, it 3) _____ easy for him to get financial help for the project, and there 4) _____ many problems. One concern 5) _____ safety. During construction, there 6) _____ a net in place under the bridge to stop people falling. As a result, there 7) _____ many fatal accidents.

Strauss 8) _____ also a poet. His most famous poem is "The Mighty Task Is Done," about the completion of the bridge.

Workbook Unit 6

4 Answer the questions about your day. Use complete sentences.

a. Where were you at 7:30 a.m. yesterday?
_____

b. Were you at school at 8:30 a.m.?
_____

c. Where were you at 11:30 a.m.?
_____

d. Where were you at 7:00 p.m.?
_____

5 Circle nine jobs.

G	I	B	S	G	A	M	F	N	Q	P	D
I	M	R	E	C	H	U	U	P	T	D	O
O	S	U	R	R	T	S	Z	O	Z	V	C
N	N	P	V	G	A	I	V	L	B	K	T
M	Q	S	E	O	X	C	M	I	L	V	O
M	X	Y	R	X	I	I	D	T	A	A	R
J	W	S	A	M	D	A	V	I	R	Z	Q
W	A	I	T	E	R	N	A	C	T	O	R
B	M	K	V	O	I	V	D	I	I	C	R
F	V	K	J	J	V	S	L	A	S	Q	A
T	E	A	C	H	E	R	D	N	T	Z	D
D	Q	Z	G	D	R	R	N	Y	J	W	U

6 Read the examples and use the words to complete the rules.

> *My sister worked in a restaurant last summer.*
> *We moved to a bigger house last summer.*
> *I studied hard and passed my math exam.*
> *My father stopped smoking last year.*
> *My parents married in a small church.*

worked   stopped   married   emigrated
moved   studied   passed

a. If the verb ends in a consonant, we add *-ed*. Examples: _____, _____

b. If the verb ends in *-e*, we add *-d*. Examples: _____, _____

c. If the verb ends in a vowel + a consonant, we double the consonant and add *-ed*.
Example: _____

d. If the verb ends in consonant + *-y*, we drop the *-y* and add *-ied*. Examples: _____, _____

Workbook Unit 6

7 Complete the sentences with the correct form of the verbs in parentheses.

a. My grandparents _____ (marry) in 1947.

b. They _____ (arrive) in the US when they were twenty-five.

c. They _____ (want) to have a better life.

d. At first, they _____ (live) in a poor part of New York.

e. My grandfather _____ (decide) to be a police officer.

f. He _____ (like) his job, but it was quite dangerous.

g. After three years, they _____ (move) to a new house and _____ (start) a family.

8 Write the past form of the verbs.

a. change: _____

b. escape: _____

c. shop: _____

d. cry: _____

e. listen: _____

f. study: _____

g. decide: _____

h. plan: _____

i. use: _____

j. drop: _____

k. practice: _____

l. worry: _____

9 Unscramble the words to form a dialogue.

MARK: to / Did / Pilgrims / travel / the / America / by ship?

_____

PROFESSOR BROWN: they / did. / Yes,

_____

MARK: they / land / in / Did / Canada?

_____

PROFESSOR BROWN: No, / they / land / Canada. / in / didn't

_____

MARK: Americans / the Pilgrims? / Native / attack / the / Did

_____

PROFESSOR BROWN: Pilgrims. / No, / attack / they / the / didn't

_____

MARK: Did / Pilgrims? / help / they / the

_____

PROFESSOR BROWN: they / did. / Yes,

_____

MARK: Americans / Pilgrims treat / Did / the / Native / well? / the

_____

PROFESSOR BROWN: Americans / didn't / No, / the Pilgrims / treat / the / Native / well.

_____

❤ Self-Assessment   Unit 6

Think about Unit 6. Write your impressions about each section of the unit.
Include what you learned and how you improved.

Unit Opener

_____
_____
_____
_____
_____
_____

My World

_____
_____
_____
_____
_____
_____

Views

_____
_____
_____
_____
_____
_____

Out and About

_____
_____
_____
_____
_____
_____
_____

❤ What do I have to do to learn more?

☐ Pay more attention in class.

☐ Do more practice exercises.

☐ Participate more in class.

☐ Study more at home.

☐ Read and listen to English in my free time.

☐ Practice writing and speaking.

☐ Other: _____

Unit 6   135

Workbook Unit 7

1 Read the summaries and match them to the genres.

adventure   comedy   horror   romance   science fiction

a. Robjo is a very smart robot. It is more intelligent than its owner, Mr. Perkins. It learns fast and soon controls all the technology in the house. But the robot wants more: Mr. Perkins' car, his house, and his family. We soon learn that Mr. Perkins is flying into space, and never coming back! _____

b. James arrives in town when his father starts working at a bank. James is charming and popular with the girls — especially Jenny. She sits next to him in biology. Soon she likes James more and more. The day of the school dance comes and she has to make a big decision. _____

c. Mr. Goblinor lives in a castle near a lake in a beautiful forest. When he gets old, his son sells the castle to a hotel company. Mr. Goblinor soon dies. Every night his ghost visits the hotel guests and plays jokes on them. One night some guests find a mouse in the bed and the next night, a snake is sleeping in the bathroom! Every day brings a funnier surprise. _____

d. Sally is on vacation with her family in Thailand. One morning, they are shopping in a street market when Sally gets lost. She looks everywhere with no luck. She is so tired that she falls asleep on a bench. When she wakes up, an old woman is speaking to Sally. She doesn't understand what the woman is saying. _____

e. The Smiths move to a new house that was built on an old cemetery. One day their son is playing in the yard when he finds a bone. He keeps it under his bed. The next day he finds more bones and he starts having bad dreams. _____

2 Read the extracts and write what the pronouns refer to.

a. "Robjo is a very smart robot. It is more intelligent than its owner, Mr. Perkins. It learns fast and soon controls all the technology in the house."

   It refers to _____ .

b. "We soon learn that Mr. Perkins is flying into space, and never coming back!"

   We refers to _____ .

c. "James is charming and popular with the girls — especially Jenny. She sits next to him in biology."

   Him refers to _____ .

d. "Every night his ghost visits the hotel guests and plays jokes on them."

   Them refers to _____ .

e. "Sally is on vacation with her family in Thailand. One morning they are shopping in a street market when she gets lost."

   They refers to _____ .

f. "When she wakes up, an old woman is speaking to Sally. She doesn't understand what the woman is saying."

   She refers to _____ .

Workbook Unit 7

3 Read the examples and use relative pronouns to complete the rule.

> A novelist is a person that writes novels.
> A library is a place where you can read books.
> Marcus is the student who won the spelling contest.
> Monopoly is a board game that I play with my family.
> I like novels that are easy to read.

In relative clauses we use _____ or _____ for people, _____ for things, and _____ for places.

4 Use *who*, *that*, or *where* to complete the sentences.

a. Is this the book _____ you are reading?
b. This is the school _____ my father studied.
c. That's the camera _____ I want for my birthday.
d. Batman is the type of superhero _____ always wins.

5 Use *who*, *that*, and *where* to write three sentences about a person, place, and thing from a book you know.

a. _____
b. _____
c. _____

6 Use the prompts to complete the sentences about what the people did.

> yesterday / stay in bed   I go to school every day but…   I didn't go to school yesterday. I stayed in bed.

a. yesterday / drink orange juice
   I drink a glass of milk for breakfast every day but…
   _____

b. yesterday / watch TV
   I meet my friends in the park after school every day but…
   _____

c. last week / take the bus
   My mother goes to work by car but…
   _____

d. last Saturday / work in the garden
   My parents see their friends on Saturdays but…
   _____

e. last Monday / forget it at home
   My sister takes her cell phone to school but…
   _____

f. last night / get home late
   My father gets home at six o'clock but…
   _____

Workbook Unit 7

7 Complete the paragraph with the correct form of the verbs.

| see | hear | go | be | fall | decide | talk | run | feel |

Last summer I 1) _____ camping with my parents. After dinner, my brother and I 2) _____ to go for a walk. We went down to the beach. It 3) _____ a warm night but it was very dark. We 4) _____ for a while but suddenly we 5) _____ something in front of us. It was enormous and it started to come towards us. "Run!" my brother shouted. I 6) _____ very fast but the sand was wet and I 7) _____ . I 8) _____ a noise and looked up. A black and white cow looked back at me! I 9) _____ really stupid.

8 Underline the correct conjunction to complete the sentences.

   a. The stories entertained people, *and/but* they taught them about their culture.

   b. Some stories were serious, *but/or* others were funny.

   c. Storytellers wanted the stories to be interesting, *but/so* they used music.

   d. The stories were popular with old people, young people, *and/but* children.

   e. During the stories, people sometimes danced *but/or* played the drums.

9 Work in pairs. Invent a story using the elements in the pictures. Use your notebook.

| a baby boy | a donkey | a pony | a tent |

10 Write sentences using the prompts with time clauses. Use commas as needed.

> when / villagers / meet / baby / they / celebrate
> When the villagers met the baby, they celebrated.

   a. chief / be / unhappy / when / he / see / donkey
   _____

   b. when / boy / sit on / donkey / he / smiled
   _____

   c. donkey / kick / when / mother / put / tent / on / it
   _____

   d. when / enemy / attack / donkey / run away
   _____

   e. parents / cry / with joy / when / see / donkey / and / boy / they
   _____

138 Unit 7

❤ Self-Assessment   Unit 7

Think about Unit 7. Write your impressions about each section of the unit.
Include what you learned and how you improved.

Unit Opener

My World

Views

Out and About

❤ What do I have to do to learn more?

☐ Pay more attention in class.   ☐ Do more practice exercises.

☐ Participate more in class.   ☐ Study more at home.

☐ Read and listen to English in my free time.   ☐ Practice writing and speaking.

☐ Other: _____

Unit 7   139

Workbook Unit 8

1 Underline the correct words to complete the sentences.

a. Fruits like strawberries and oranges contain a lot of *endorphins/vitamin C*.

b. Carrots, onions, and peas are *fruit/vegetables*.

c. Vitamin C is good for your *teeth/skin* and bones.

d. Chocolate needs to be at least 70 percent pure *cocoa/milk* to get the full effect of endorphins.

e. Bananas make us feel energetic because they contain *potassium/iron* and natural sugars.

f. Spinach is rich in vitamin B, which helps fight *depression/stress*.

g. Pure chocolate increases the level of endorphins in our *brain/skin*.

2 Complete the exchange with *some* or *any*.

A: So, what are you going to make?

B: A strawberry smoothie. It's very easy. You need 1) _____ strawberries, 2) _____ milk and 3) _____ ice.

A: Do you need 4) _____ sugar?

B: Well, you don't need 5) _____ sugar but you can use 6) _____ if you want to make it a bit sweeter.

A: Do we have 7) _____ strawberries in the refrigerator?

B: Yes, we do, and there's also 8) _____ milk.

A: What about ice?

B: Let me see… there isn't 9) _____ ice but there is 10) _____ ice cream.

A: Why don't we eat strawberries and ice cream?

B: That's a good idea!

3 Write sentences about what Andy bought in the supermarket.

> apples
> He bought some apples.
>
> bananas
> He didn't buy any bananas.

a. oranges
_____

b. watermelon
_____

c. carrots
_____

d. chocolate
_____

e. lemonade
_____

f. rice
_____

g. chips
_____

Subject
apples ✓
bananas ✗
oranges ✓
a watermelon ✗
carrots ✓
chocolate ✗
lemonade ✓
rice ✓
chips ✗

140 Unit 8

Workbook Unit 8

4 Check your refrigerator and answer the questions.

a. Is there any fruit? What kind?
_____

b. Are there any vegetables? What kind?
_____

c. Is there any soda?
_____

d. Is there any ice cream?
_____

e. Is there any meat?
_____

f. Is there any fish?
_____

5 Read the text and circle the correct options to complete the rules.

> My classmates are all very talented.
> Gary is a good chess player. He plays very well and he learns quickly.
> Clara dances beautifully. She is a great dancer.
> Bill speaks German fluently. He speaks German more fluently than he speaks Portuguese.
> I love running but I don't run very fast.

a. Adjectives describe *people and things/actions*.

b. Adverbs describe *people and things/actions*.

c. We normally add **-ly** to an *adverb/adjective* to form an *adverb/adjective*.

d. Some adverbs like **well**, **fast**, and **hard** are *regular/irregular*.

e. Adverbs of manner go *after/before* the verb in a sentence.

6 Look at the pictures and use adverbs of manner to write sentences describing what the people are doing and how they are doing it.

Phil

Mike

Steve

Julie

Phil runs *quickly*.   _____   _____   _____

_____   _____   _____   _____

Workbook Unit 8

7 Write sentences describing the weather in the cities.

What's the weather like today in…?

New York City	It's cold and rainy in New York City.
Phoenix	
Chicago	
Anchorage	
Los Angeles	

8 Use the prompts to write the conversations between the people in the pictures.

a.

b.

what / matter?

_____

headache / fever

_____

why / go home and rest

_____

you / feeling OK?

_____

no / stomachache

_____

How about / go to the doctor

_____

9 Check the correct reply to each sentence.

a. I'm really tired.
   ____ Why don't you have a sandwich?
   ____ Why don't you go to bed?
   ____ Let's go out.

b. Why don't we play tennis?
   ____ OK, that's a good idea.
   ____ No, I'm not hungry.
   ____ Yes. What movie shall we see?

c. Shall we make a pizza?
   ____ No, there isn't any milk in the fridge.
   ____ No, we had some for lunch.
   ____ No, it's going to rain.

d. Let's go shopping.
   ____ No, it's too cold to play.
   ____ Yes, shall we order a pizza?
   ____ That's a good idea. I want to get a pair of jeans.

❯ Self-Assessment — Unit 8

Think about Unit 8. Write your impressions about each section of the unit. Include what you learned and how you improved.

Unit Opener

_____
_____
_____
_____
_____
_____
_____

My World

_____
_____
_____
_____
_____
_____
_____

Views

_____
_____
_____
_____
_____
_____
_____

Out and About

_____
_____
_____
_____
_____
_____
_____

❯ What do I have to do to learn more?

- ☐ Pay more attention in class.
- ☐ Do more practice exercises.
- ☐ Participate more in class.
- ☐ Study more at home.
- ☐ Read and listen to English in my free time.
- ☐ Practice writing and speaking.
- ☐ Other: _____

Book 2

Publisher
Lauren Robbins

Series Editor
Simon Cupit, Ana Luiza Couto

Editors
Arnoldo Langner Romero, Imelda Vazquez Córdova, Jorge Mancera Cardós, Mariana Albertini

Authors
Michael Downie, David Gray, Juan Manuel Jimenez

Proofreading
Aaron Burkholder, Angélica Soares

Series Design
Daniela Ibarra

Cover Design
Gilciane Munhoz, João Brito, Carla Almeida Freire

Cover Illustration
Indio San

Design Coordination
Daniela Ibarra

Layout and DTP
Daniela Ibarra, Rocío Echávarri R.

Illustration
Antonio Rocha, David Peón, Diego Omar Uriarte

Photography
© iStockphoto, 2017
© Fotolia, 2017
© Latinstock, 2017
© AFP, 2017
© Getty Images, 2017
© Other Images, 2017
© Shutterstock, 2018
© Pulsar Imagens, 2018

Production
Ulisses Pires, Juliano de Arruda Fernandes, Ivan Toledo

Picture Research
Josiane Laurentino, Susan Eiko

The trademark University of Dayton Publishing is the property of University of Dayton. Unauthorized copying, reproduction, hiring, and lending prohibited.

U.D. Publishing, S.A. de C.V., is the exclusive licensee of the University of Dayton Publishing brand.

University of Dayton
300 College Park
Dayton, OH 45469

i-World 2
Student's Book & Workbook / Teacher's Book
First edition, 2018
© U.D. Publishing, S.A. de C.V., México.
All rights reserved.
br.educamos.sm

Dados Internacionais de Catalogação na Publicação (CIP)
(Câmara Brasileira do Livro, SP, Brasil)

Downie, Michael
  i-world 2 : student's book & workbook / teacher's book
    Michael Downie, David Gray, Juan Manuel Jimenez. —
  São Paulo : Edições SM, 2018.

  Inclui CD.
  ISBN 978-85-418-2019-6 (S.B.)
  ISBN 978-85-418-2023-3 (T.B.)

  1. Inglês (Ensino fundamental) I. Gray, David.
II. Jimenez, Juan Manuel. III. Título.

18-15015   CDD-372.652

Índices para catálogo sistemático:
1. Inglês : Ensino fundamental 372.652

Iolanda Rodrigues Biode - Bibliotecária - CRB-8/10014

All rights reserved. No part of this book may be reproduced, stored in a retrieval system, or transmitted in any form or by any means, electronic, mechanical, photocopying, recording or otherwise, without prior permission in writing of the publishers.

Printed in Brazil/*Impresso no Brasil*

i-World 2
Student's Book & Workbook / Teacher's Book
Printed in April 2018 at Ricargraf

Rua Tenente Lycurgo Lopes da Cruz, 55
Água Branca 05036-120 São Paulo SP Brasil
Tel. 11 2111-7400
edicoessm@grupo-sm.com
www.edicoessm.com.br